Individuality and Primal Unity: Ego's Struggle for Dominance in Today's World

by Jim Willis

Volume I: Ego and Earth Magic
(*Merlin the Magician: A Mystery for the Ages*)

Volume II: Ego and the Hero
(*Robin Hood: Victory Through Defiance*)

Volume III: Ego and Innocence
(*Little Snow-White: A Road Map for Our Time*)

Individuality and Primal Unity: Ego's Struggle for
Dominance in Today's World - Volume III: Ego and
Innocence (*Little Snow-White: A Road Map for Our Time*)
© 2021 Jim Willis
ISBN: 978-1-989940-33-4
Dimensionfold Publishing

Preface

At some point in the distant past, a remote, ancient ancestor began to think in terms of the word "I." He or she became the first to understand the concept of individuality — the idea that "I" am separate and distinct from "You" and harbor different needs and desires. In that moment, *Ego* was born and humankind was metaphorically cast out of Eden. The struggle for existence, now understood in terms of a struggle for individual survival, began. No longer was identity found in species recognition. The "One" became the "Many." Unity was fractured. Henceforth the individual would reign supreme. "Look out for #1" became a human mantra and the quest for individual power began.

It continues to this day. Ego didn't necessarily lose the ability to feel empathy and compassion, but from the very beginning its primary instincts were for personal protection, survival, and growth. This has led to such concepts as the divine right of kings, class warfare, political dominance, top-heavy economic control over the means of industrial production, and monetary benefits for the few as opposed to the many.

Especially in these days of social media, every morning it has become standard procedure for many people to stare into the allegorical mirror of their computer screen, affirm their social status based on the number of responses they generated overnight, and ask, "Who is the fairest of them all?" It would appear as though Snow-White's evil stepmother has been reincarnated and lives on in modern society. Increasingly, we find ourselves living in Ego's home country, a land called Narcissism.

How do we resist such an insidious enemy? As always, those who came before left us clues to follow. Their wisdom forms the basis of this trilogy.

Those who created the old, familiar myths, legends, and bedtime tales were well aware of the dangers of Ego. They might not have understood the struggle in modern, psychological terms. But they were intuitive enough to compose stories about it. In these imaginative tales they pitted Ego against the healing magic of Earth Energy, the ancestral Eden from whence Ego had sprung.

Eventually, the civilized "Ego of the City" sought to destroy its wild and untamed predecessor who still lived out in the natural world. It is not by accident that the biblical story begins in a Genesis garden and ends in a Revelation city. It is revealing when Hebrew mythology records that right after the first murder was perpetrated because of a bruised ego, the murderer, Cain, went out and built a city east of Eden. Ever since, the metaphorical story of civilization is the story of the power struggle between cities. Industrial civilization, not the army, destroyed the American Indians. Today's headlines remind us again and again that the technology of development is a two-edged sword. Urban blight is a principle enemy of nature's resources. These stories mark the progress of Ego's conquests.

We will explore this subject by means of an in-depth analysis of three ancient tales. Each story will be developed in a separate book which can stand alone on its own, but will be part of a trilogy that encompasses the three stages of Ego's rise to dominance.

Part I: Ego and Earth Magic (*Merlin the Magician: A Mystery for the Ages*)

In the Arthurian legends, Merlin the Magician is pitted against dark energies summoned by Ego, who seeks to destroy the source of ancient Earth Magic. At the end, Ego appears to be victorious. Merlin is presented as the last of the old ones to be associated with natural magic, and is entombed in a crystal cave, deep in the bowels of the earth.

But just as in the Christ story, the Arthurian tale of the *Once and Future King*, the American Indian Tecumseh legends, and the Tolkien Ring Cycle, there is the promise of a return. Merlin will one day awake to be reunited with Arthur. The union of Earth Magic and spiritual Camelot will be spread abroad "on earth, as it is in heaven."

Until then, however, with ancient Earth Magic seemingly destroyed, or at least imprisoned, Ego is free to strike out at those humans who still follow the old, earth-based, natural ways.

Part II: Ego and the Hero (*Robin Hood: Victory Through Defiance*)

The Hero, Robin Hood, is a nature man who is at home in the wild forests of Sherwood. He defies the ego-centric, power-hungry sheriff of Nottingham, who remains ensconced in his fortified urban castle. In the end, the Hero teaches us to be victorious by defying Ego's claims on personal freedom and individual choice. Robin Hood refuses walls and the loss of independence. His final victory is assured with the return of King Richard, and his marriage to Marian reunites nature and civilization into one spiritual landscape.

Part III: Ego and Innocence (*Little Snow-White: A Road Map for Our Time*)

In the story of *Little Snow-White*, Queen Ego, secure in her castle, seeks to destroy Snow-White, who represents Intuitive Innocence. Snow-White lives in the wild forest "across the seven mountains" with the seven dwarfs. In the end, Innocence triumphs over Ego through her interaction with earth energies. As in the story of Robin Hood, once victory is assured, her marriage to the prince from a faraway, mysterious land, unites the physical and the spiritual aspects of life in our perception realm. (Spoiler alert: Awakening Snow-White with a kiss is a Disney abomination. In the original version, she awakens through interaction with Earth Energy!)

In the first tale, Earth Magic is seemingly neutralized and imprisoned in the crystal cave of the earth. This is a picture of 21st century life. Civilization has brought about a feeling of deadness when it comes to the natural world. We have separated ourselves from the very Earth Mother who gave us birth. Ego can never-the-less be defeated by energies and forces inherent in the natural world. Therein lies our hope and our salvation. Earth Energy slumbers, but is not defeated. Not yet.

In the next two stories we explore the current status of Ego in today's world. It battles both the Hero and the Innocent, but Earth Magic still comes to the aid of the deserving if we are attuned to its beckoning call.

All three stories reach their climax when hope arrives in the guise of "Royalty" from outside, a reference to spiritual help that is always available to those who are in touch with nature. In the case of Merlin, spiritual aid comes from Arthur the King. Robin Hood welcomes the return of King Richard. Snow-White is joined by the mysterious prince. None of these visitors arrives to "save the day." Rather, they make their entrance after the battle is already won. Their presence may have been subtle and understated, but their ancient magic and power was none the less available.

So it is that in our civilized world, invented and dominated by materialistic Ego, selfish individuality often appears to be victorious, while archaic Earth Magic seems imprisoned in a tomb. But in the end, spiritual energies from the natural world, which is a manifestation of the Source of All That Is, offers the hope of triumph over seemingly impossible odds.

Individualistic Ego's demise, we are assured, is certain, and the unity of Eden will again be restored when spirituality arrives in the flesh to participate in the final victory.

In the end, this is a trilogy of hope.

Little Snow-White:

A Road Map for Our Time

Jim Willis

Dedication

This book is dedicated to Ken Goudsward,
who saw spiritual growth where others saw only
commercial marketability,
and thus restored *Little Snow White* back to life.
Thanks, Ken!

Table of Contents

Introduction

Science vs. religion. Religion vs. spirituality. Spirituality vs. intuition. Intuition vs. intellect. And underneath it all, us versus them.

Sometimes it seems as though the search for meaning in contemporary life has become a battlefield. Heated words and dogmatic phrases dominate the conversation in the decreasing instances when conversation is even engaged. Opposing camps hunker down in their bunkers and lob verbal bombs at each other, usually delivered via the Internet. There is no need for contestants in this war to look each other in the eye. They can deliver their missiles of hate and disdain right from their desktops, delivering digital drones that seek out and destroy with wholesale destruction.

Long gone are the days, if they ever really existed, when a good religious/spiritual discussion was something to be sought out and savored. Now, if we are to follow Mark Twain's advice, it is far better to avoid any mention of religion, or even spirituality, in polite company. It serves only to divide.

Many years ago, I took a bicycle trip, exploring the entire length of the Connecticut River from its source in a small beaver pond just south of the Canadian/New Hampshire border all the way down to where it emptied into Long Island Sound. In those days the border guards were quite different than they are today. I had intended to start at the US border itself, thinking that the maps were correct in identifying the source of the river as Fourth Connecticut Lake, just south of the border in New Hampshire. But when I told the lonely Canadian customs officer what I was doing, he insisted that I leave my bike with him and hike a few hundred yards through the Canadian woods back to the small swamp that marked the real source of the river. He thought it would be a shame to bike the entire river and not see the exact spot where it began. The memory of his kindness and helpfulness has always stayed with me. He reached out to a stranger, and made a friend. I'm sure he doesn't remember me, but I will always remember him and his simple act of thoughtfulness.

I was soon to be reminded, however, of quite the opposite experience.

About a hundred miles into my trip, I passed an historic landmark that marked the spot where the Second

Congregational Church in a particular town once stood. It had long since burned down. Less than a quarter mile later I passed another sign that memorialized the location of the First Congregational Church, which had also disappeared into the mists of time.

My curiosity was peaked. Why would a small New England town need two Congregational churches, less than a half-mile mile apart?

Being by nature a curious researcher, when I got to the town and discovered a small library, I just had to stop and ask some questions. The helpful librarian directed me to a local history book which, low and behold, answered my question. It seems that a hundred years ago the congregants of the First Congregational Church got into a furious theological argument over whether or not animals had souls and went to heaven when they died. The discussion grew so heated that half the congregation felt the need to leave and start their own church. Hence, the Second Congregational Church, located a quarter of a mile away from the First.

Since then, I have often wondered about what some bewildered and unsuspecting family who had just moved into town must have felt when they were paid the requisite visit from two local pastors who proceeded to force them to make a decision about a subject that probably had never even occurred to them. The weddings of future sons and daughters, the baptisms of their subsequent children, the choice of local casseroles at church dinners, and the final resting place of Aunt Maude, for generations to come, would all rest on their answer to the thorny question, "Where did Fido go when he died?"

Of such is the kingdom of heaven.

Religion, Spirituality, and Mythology

As funny as that experience was, and it gave me a lot to think about for the rest of the trip, it is dwarfed by the religious warfare and hatred that now engulfs the world. Religions that preach against "taking the Lord's name in vain" seem to be quite good at narrowing their definition of what "in vain" means when they invoke a divine entity to aid them in destroying someone who doesn't share their ideologies.

How did we get into this mess? And more important, how do we get out of it?

Perhaps the answer lies in a wisdom that predates any of the established texts of the current world religions. It might even go back as far as our remote, ancient ancestors, who had for untold millennia been dealing with thorny issues of life and death, of how to live an authentic, meaningful life in a troubling world, and how to explore the intricate landscape of soul and spirit while living in a material world. If information from ancient temples, such as 11,000-year-old Göbekli Tepe and a possibly human-constructed pyramid complex called Gunung Padang, which is even 12,000 years older than that, are being interpreted correctly, spirituality and questions about life, death, and meaning, go way, way back in time.

I'm talking, of course, about mythology. Joseph Campbell taught the modern world that myths are maps that offer clues on our journey through life. They are guides that tell us we don't have to reinvent the wheel when it comes to spirituality. Others have gone before us. The road is explored and well-marked. All we have to do is follow the signposts.

If religion has become a cause of dissension among us, maybe the way out of the morass is to go back before religions formed, to the essential experience of the ancient ones. We learn from religious texts that Abraham, Moses, the Buddha, Jesus, Mohammad, and many, many more wisdom teachers, all experienced the supernatural in a vivid way. They all emerged from their experience with a new vision. But this essential vision was later turned into a tradition by those who built the world religions that now seem to have strayed far away from their initial inspiration. Followers of such traditions are now often corralled with strict dogmas and doctrines, imprisoned within pastures where spirit once roamed free and wild.

This tendency is not restricted to religious organizations. In the field of psychology, followers of Freud and followers of Jung hunker down behind their self-imposed barriers and viciously attack each other. They, in turn, suffer the barbs and arrows of Rogerians and new age eclectics.

Moving to the field of physics, Albert Einstein had a long-standing feud with Niels Bohr. Their followers are well-known for vicious attacks that have even led to suicides by those ostracized and forced out of the halls of academia. Sad to say, the ideas of some of those who died before their time were subsequently proved to be correct.

The world of academic archeology has a similar history. A quick perusal of Wikipedia reveals the on-line encyclopedia to be a fierce battleground of opposing ideas. Adherents often use phrases such as "completely discredited" and "totally destroyed" when it comes to sarcastic and malicious attacks aimed at those who hold rival opinions.

What's a poor seeker to do when it comes time to look for a path that leads to inward exploration and spiritual truth? Anywhere they turn they find only hostility and malice.

A long time ago, a time span measured in perhaps thousands of years, experienced elders taught young people by telling stories. Stories make us think. They resonate with us because we bring our own experience to them. We identify. We recognize that the truth discovered by the hero of a story is powerful because it represents our own, personal quest.

Go back in time to an age where an inward, personal, earth-based, natural way of nomadic life was rapidly being replaced by an increasingly regimented, eventually mechanized, agricultural society that functioned best when people were told what to do rather than allowed the freedom to find their own way. Civilization works best when people know their place and march in lock-step. Wild, uncontrolled flights of fantasy are discouraged because they are not dependable. When our individual acceptance is based on imposed custom rather than an inward compass, we tend to seek approval from others and start to lose our own, authentic path. Ego comes to the fore. We want to be number one! We seek that position by overpowering others so that we can prove that we have triumphed over something important. Competition becomes everything. Rather than being proud of a potential rival's success, we look inside ourselves and find only envy. If you win, I lose, so I'm jealous.

Like it or not, this form of living and being has conquered virtually every corner of the modern, industrialized world. It has become the gospel of the materialistic age, preached by victors from the fields of sports, entertainment, politics, academia, and religious institutions. We are trained in its precepts since birth, told that we must attend the best schools, live in the best neighborhoods, and mingle with the best social groups. Egos develop to outlandish size and our true, spiritual natures retreat into hibernation.

Sad to say, most people today probably have no comprehension of all this, and cannot even imagine the price we have paid for conformity. We observe the ascendance of conditions such as depression, sickness, anxiety, emotional suffering, remorse, hatred, and discouragement, not knowing that they are all symptoms of one disease. Spiritual malaise.

The ancients recognized this. The old ones saw it coming. They recognized the signs of a new age on the horizon and realized intuitively that it carried both a blessing and a curse.

How did they warn us of the pitfalls? As always, they told stories. Their stories were passed down from generation to generation. Eventually they were written down. It is probable that those who finally recorded the stories had long since forgotten what they were really about.

Deep-seated wisdom became submerged under fanciful tales for children. "Fairytales," they were called. "Bed-time stories" for children. And then came the cruelest cut of all. Walt Disney made them cute. Once a rich, deep, well-thought-out and carefully constructed wisdom teaching becomes a cartoon, nobody takes it seriously anymore. Heigh ho, heigh ho, it's off to irrelevance we go. And no one stops to realize that the very wisdom needed desperately by an ailing society populated by people filled with despair has been hiding in plain sight for lo these many centuries.

Treasure Troves of Wisdom

The story of *Little Snow-White* is such a source of wisdom. It offers seekers today everything they need to get back on the path to spiritual healing. Our journey together as we explore this story will focus on recapturing the ancient, deeply relevant, and spiritually enriching message that the ancients intuitively knew would be needed as an age of individual freedom evolved into an age of connected, controlled, dependent civilization.

Since time often travels in circles, this is a message whose time has come once again. We, too, are living in an age of change. The recent age of conformity and industrial technology is, right before our eyes, opening up into an age of individual chaos and wild abandon. The very technology meant to make us a connected and unified whole has instead ushered in an age of individual possibility and advancement. A generation trained by the military to follow orders and march together has morphed into a generation which strives to, in the words of Frank Sinatra, "do it my way." Is it any wonder that conservatism is hunkering down in fear and circling its wagons, certain that a remembered age which was golden in memory, if not in fact, is being threatened? All around the world people long for the good old days, even though those days were good for only a privileged few.

"The times, they are a changin'," sang Bob Dylan. And, like all prophets, although he may have been a few years ahead of the algorithm, he was absolutely right. Signs of the times are everywhere for those who have eyes to see. People are confused. People are worried. People are depressed. This is to be expected. The world of top-heavy control is shifting to individuals who can now communicate ideas directly to each other without waiting for official approval.

Politicians have discovered that they can't cover things up as they once did. Ike Eisenhower and John Kennedy may have been blessed with a press corps that tacitly agreed to cover up their sexual indiscretions, but Bill Clinton and Donald Trump were not. US Steel may once have been able to get away with manipulating overseas deals, but Facebook can't. You can no longer hoodwink a gullible public if that public is armed with the power of Twitter.

It's true that ideas concerning personal choice are still up in the air and no one is quite sure where they will land. The new world of individual freedom is similar to a wild frontier. People can still be manipulated into voting a certain way if a foreign power cleverly learns to use its formidable digital powers to subtly infiltrate the minds and hearts of blocks of voters who haven't quite caught up to new paradigms. Then those foreign digital techniques are weaponized by domestic organizations that utilize them against voters from the opposing political party. And the wheels on the bus go round and round. We have a long way to go.

But that is precisely when old wisdom becomes so important. There is nothing new under the sun. People are still people, subject to the same feelings and emotions that have affected us since the beginning of time. We still worry about life and death. We still struggle with how to live an authentic life within a troubling culture. We still wonder how to explore the intricate maze of soul and spirit while imbedded in a material world.

The familiar version of *Little Snow-White* was first published by the brothers Grimm in 1812, although the story itself is undoubtedly much older than that. The world of their day was steeped in political upheaval and unrest. Old alliances were breaking apart. Technology was changing the established way of doing things. A new day was dawning and no one quite knew what to expect. It was, in many important ways, similar to what we face today.

But wisdom is timeless. The old lessons still ring true. They are needed now more than ever. If we think we are somehow unique and special and that nothing like this has ever happened before, we are historically blind and guilty of the sin of hubris. Why struggle to find a new path when the old one is right before us, although perhaps a bit overgrown with weeds and disuse?

The task that now lies before us is to cut through the weeds and rediscover the wisdom of those who already made a transition similar to the one that now faces us. This is what they were trying to tell us in *Little Snow-White*. It is a story of innocent intuition being overwhelmed by consuming ego. The archetypes found here are universal. Snow-White sleeps within each of us, and longs to be awakened. The story tells us how to wake her from her poisoned slumber. It perfectly describes our current situation, and is as relevant as this morning's news feed.

What might happen in our world when our inner Snow-White awakens to a new day and recognizes a familiar cultural landscape? What are the possibilities?

Let's find out together.

The Map Legend

Every map has a legend, an explanation of the symbols it uses and some useful information about who put it together and printed it. This chapter is such a legend and explores how the story of *Little Snow-White* came to be.

First of all, no one knows how old this tale is or how far back in time its genesis really lies.

Joseph Campbell believed it to be a remnant of what he calls "high culture" myths. By this he meant that he believed myths to be the result of an intellectual elite who transcended the common people of their day when it came to art, poetry, music, dance, or cultural norms.

Robert Bly thought, as do I, that the origins of these kinds of stories can be traced all the way back to shamanism, before the agricultural revolution and the rise of so-called "higher" civilizations. Perhaps they even predate what we call "our" civilization, going back to ancient cultures that passed on their wisdom before they tragically disappeared. If this is the case, they are valuable indeed, because they originated with very ancient peoples who learned the hard way what life is all about and, like a venerable, elder grandfather or grandmother, wanted to pass on what they had learned before they died.

Marie-Louise von Franz, a Swiss Jungian psychologist and scholar, taught that what she called Fairy Tales resulted from those who experienced paranormal or parapsychological journeys into what we now call the soul or psyche. Heavily influenced by Carl Jung and his theories about archetypes, she searched out their roots in the classic experience of deep psychological exploration.

The Shamanic Experience

Perhaps the most insightful way of exploring the origins of myth and fairy tales involves turning to what I like to call the shamanic experience. When shamans, using a variety of trance-inducing techniques, actually encounter extra-dimensional beings who grant them instructions, healing methods, and wisdom, they bring these teachings back for the benefit of their "tribes." This would explain the animal-human hybrids so often associated with shamanic journeying, or the ability of animals found in nature to speak in human language or engage in human-like mannerisms. Such experiences, being deeply entwined with nature and animal envoys, often speak of unifying connections in these terms. Mythology is full of such entities, which are called therianthropes. They are found painted on cave walls and pecked into rock art. Egyptian murals, Mayan depictions, and Chinese pictures prominently feature them. They are found in the Old Testament of the Bible.

Probably because ancient people lived much closer to nature than we do, the farther back in time we go, the more we find them. Although specific therianthropes are not found in Snow-White, nature figures prominently in this tale. So, we have to be alert to nature themes and shamanic images.

Setting the Stage

However the tale of *Little Snow-White* originated, it was first popularized by the brothers Grimm. Jacob and Wilhelm Grimm were aptly named. Some of their tales make for pretty grim reading, especially if you read them to your kids before they go to bed at night. The violence and explicit scenes can lead to nightmares.

In 1819 they cleaned Snow-White up a little. In the original 1812 version, Snow-White's own mother poisoned her. The 1819 version changed it to a wicked step-mother. Disney, of course, scrubbed it up even more. His 1937 film made no mention of the fact that at the end the wicked queen was forced to put on red-hot iron shoes and dance herself to death. Early editions even describe her heels and toes being cut off to fit inside the shoes. This is definitely not your run of the mill, kiddy entertainment that we like to view today. If Disney's cartoon had included an episode like this it would never have been given the Good Housekeeping seal of approval.

On the assumption, though, that the earlier version of the tale was probably closer to the truth of the original story, I'm going to cite the earliest possible version in the pages to follow. Let the chips fall where they may. There is usually a reason for the violence we will encounter. It's meant to shock us into awareness.

First Premise: Snow White = Intuitive Innocence = Primal Soul

First, my basic interpretive premises.

Little Snow-White presents a description of the intuitive innocence that sleeps within each of us. To make things easier to understand, from now on I'll call it the Primal Soul.

Primal Soul is our essential life force. It is the eternal energy that came from the Source and will return to the Source upon the death of our material body. It is open, receptive, curious, and responsive. It does not "think" as much as it feels. It is intuitive, and constantly seeks to explore new ideas and enter into new experiences.

In describing Primal Soul, I would love to use a descriptive word such as "virgin," were that not such a loaded concept. We associate virginity with gender, and *Little Snow-White* has little to do with *our* concepts of male and female, although it has everything to do with *the* concept of male and female.

This has to be made clear right at the beginning. When I talk about feminine energy and masculine energy, I'm not talking about biological men and women. Physical men and women are simply material expressions of the yin and yang of cosmic energy that form the basic, dualistic, creative force that pervades the cosmos. When you peek beneath biology, you soon discover that each and every one of us, indeed, each and every cell in our body and each sub-atomic particle in the universe, demonstrates this duality. It is the driving force of creation. That's why sex is so powerful and, down through the ages, has been hedged in and regulated by rules and regulations, both stated and unstated.

Sex is the desire for spiritual union that was necessarily severed when our Primal Soul chose to enter into human life where it could explore and experience individual freedom and opportunity. Deep down inside us we yearn to once again return to that spiritual unity, but realize we cannot until the time of exploration and education that we call life has ended. Nevertheless, divine unity is still part of us, even if we have temporarily forgotten it. Why else have people been known to exclaim, "My God!" at the point of sexual climax? At that point of union, we briefly remember what it was to be united in the timeless One.

What all this means is that every single one of us exhibits both feminine and masculine energy. It is true that our culture, which often perversely elevates division over unity, tries to teach us that men are completely different from women. Such division allows one gender to overpower the other. It does so by emphasizing differences, such as introducing clichés such as "women's intuition" or "it's a man's world" into our vocabulary. This is a perversion. We are all male and female, despite our gender and sexual preference.

So, when I talk about Snow-White representing intuitive innocence, or the feminine energy that sleeps within each of us, I really *mean* "each of us." Our gender has nothing to do with it, unless we heed the siren call of a misled culture and allow superficiality to dominate our thinking.

Second Premise: Wicked Queen = Ego Identity

This immediately leads to my second interpretive premise. If Snow-White represents our Primal Soul, eternal and divine, the wicked queen represents our Ego.

Ego is all about individuality and separateness. You'll notice as we continue together that the first letter of the word Ego is usually capitalized. There's a reason for this. Ego is often a proper name. It has an identity of its own. When let out of its cage, it becomes a fallen angel, the demon who wants to conquer and triumph. Rather than seek unity and one-ness, it wants to stand alone in the end zone of life, spike a football hard onto the turf of the natural world, bruising the very skin of the mother who gave us birth, lift a single finger to the skies, and shout, "I'm number 1!" Used in this way, Ego is not something we have. It is someone we become, if we allow it to take over our identity.

Ego is all about power, recognition, and individual accomplishment. Why does it so fear the Primal Soul which sleeps within? Because it recognizes that its life span is limited. When the body dies, Ego dies. As such, it spends its time prowling the world like a hungry lion, looking for food and nourishment so it can be sustained as long as possible. It is, quite literally, deathly afraid: that is, afraid of death. It knows its time is short, limited to a human life span.

In the story of *Little Snow-White*, both Primal Soul and Ego are represented by female figures. But that doesn't mean that male energy is absent. As we shall see when we begin to unroll the narrative, male energy seeks, in different and diverse ways, to lend a hand and sometimes offer help. But we enter the domain of the material creation through the womb of the Earth Mother, so it is only appropriate that the ancients presented the central figures of this particular story as contrasting women.

Other stories feature the trials and tribulations of male energy. One has only to read about mythical figures such as Atlas, Sisyphus, Odysseus, and Hercules, in order to explore the realm of male energy. But those tales are for another time. What concerns us now is the relationship between the sleeping Primal Source and the powerful and controlling Ego.

Method of Study: Exegesis

Our method of study together will involve a practice called *exegesis*. That is simply a technical term that refers to the process of critically examining the words and phrases of a particular text in order to determine why the author chose, often without conscious decision, to use some words and not others.

It's a method often used in studying and expounding religious texts, but it can be, and often is, used in other contexts. Supreme Court justices, for instance, are often called to exegete the individual words used in the United States Constitution so that they can determine exactly what the founding fathers meant when they penned a particular phrase. When the founding fathers referred to something called "due process," for instance, or "unlawful search and seizure," what did they really mean?

That's the method we'll use to try to unravel what was in the minds of the elders who first developed the story of *Little Snow-White*. Why did they formulate the characters the way they did? This story obviously grew with the telling. Each story teller probably nuanced his version a little as he or she grew more familiar with the basic idea. This is the beauty of oral culture over written culture. Once something is captured by the printed word, it stops evolving.

But this is important. Stories such as *Little Snow-White* need to be read on many different levels. Just because I may speak in terms of "this means this" and "that means that" doesn't mean I am presenting *the* interpretation. I'm merely presenting *an* interpretation. My hope is that you will see levels I have missed, or come to understand meaning that is unique to you. If you experience an "Aha!" moment that resonates with your particular life journey, that's all for the best. I will try as hard as I can to keep my own Ego at bay so that, together, we can enter into an experience of discovery that will awaken the sleeping Primal Soul within us. Only then will Snow-White live in the sunlight.

Let's begin.

THE TEXT

Once upon a time in midwinter, when the snowflakes were falling like feathers from heaven, a queen sat sewing at her window, which had a frame of black ebony wood. As she sewed, she looked up at the snow and pricked her finger with her needle. Three drops of blood fell into the snow. The red on the white looked so beautiful that she thought to herself, "If only I had a child as white as snow, as red as blood, and as black as the wood in this frame."

Soon afterward she had a little daughter who was as white as snow, as red as blood, and as black as ebony wood, and therefore she called her Little Snow-White.

Chapter 1: Separation

Once upon a time in midwinter,

when the snowflakes were falling like

feathers from heaven...

When a painter begins to produce a work of art, she begins by preparing her canvass. She covers it with a neutral color so that every added bit of pigment can be seen and utilized for what it truly is. What better neutral color is there than white? Specifically, the white of a mid-winter snowfall.

Just so in this case. Our artist begins her oral picture by first covering all the blemishes, bumps, and baubles of the world outside with a mid-winter snowfall. The scene is prepared so that nature itself, the Earth Mother in all her glory, will become the backdrop for our story. But it's not just any snowfall that prepares the world to receive the lessons that await us. It's a snowfall consisting of *"snowflakes falling like feathers from heaven."* This is an indication that the story we are about to read is special. It is a divine tale straight from heaven.

Perhaps that is why the scene is set in midwinter. The nights then are the longest of the year. It's a time for hibernating, A time for sleep. A time for dreams. So as we imagine the voice of the elder, we are immediately tipped off to the fact that the tale we are about to hear is a mystical, dream-like, divine story. We are therefore encouraged to listen especially carefully. This is no ordinary message. It comes straight from the heavenly muse.

White is a color that carries great significance. It sometimes appears as silver. Every biblical word-picture of God informs us that He (in the Bible, the masculine pronoun is almost invariably employed) has hair "as white as wool." Thus, the familiar Michelangelo murals picture God as an old man with white hair, sitting on a throne.

This is an indication that by the time even the first books of the Bible were written down, some 500 years before the common era, the masculine patriarchy was already firmly entrenched, because in mythology, some of which predates even this early era, white and silver are almost always used to represent moon energy—female energy. That flies in the face of any theology that claims God is only male.

So it is that with these opening words we are ushered into an ancient, dream-world landscape, pulsing with female energy, ready to hear a message that comes not from the lips of a human story teller, but from the Muse herself. The canvas is prepared. The palette is ready. The story begins.

... a queen sat sewing at her window, which had a frame of black ebony wood.

Right away we are met with a startling observation. Having prepared us for a nature story, even going so far as to prepare the canvass outside with a neutral color, we are told that the first character we meet is not out *in* nature, but inside, looking *out* at it through a window—with a contrasting window frame at that. The snow outside is white. When we learn the window frame is made of "*black ebony,*" we cannot help but notice a great contrast.

Inside, outside. White and black. It is a picture of duality. This is to be a story about opposites. Perhaps that gives us our first clue as to the identity of the queen who sits at the window, gazing out at nature. She is not a part of it. She has become separated from it.

33

When we consider this first clue, the story immediately hints of separation. In western cultures, a prime myth about separation is found in the story of Eden. It begins in a garden, but not just any garden. It is the primal garden—the garden of wholeness. Man and woman are one with nature, one with each other and one with God. There is no separation, no duality. They have not yet put on clothes, a potent symbol of their material bodies. It is a spiritual, mystical scene, in which God walks in the garden in the cool of the evening, conversing with Primal Souls before the so-called "fall." It pictures One-ness.

But in perfect unity there can be no growth. We are left with a feeling of incompleteness, of stagnation. Everything is the same, all the time. We might as well face the fact. Perfect unity, with no opportunity for growth, can become quite boring. A perfectly white landscape offers no contrasts. Once you get used to the view, there is nothing new to see.

In the Eden myth, it is the serpent who gets things moving. Duality exists in the garden, but only in potential. There is a tree, for instance, that offers the knowledge of good and evil. Those are polar opposites. But no one has yet sampled it, so for all practical purposes it might not even exist.

The serpent is not satisfied with the status quo. It has to grow or die. It must shed its old skin and grow a new one in order to accommodate its next larger size.

So it is with humans. How can there be growth if everything stays the same? Unity is comforting, but can there be real comfort without at least the knowledge of discomfort? Unity is joyful. But can there be joy without sorrow? It's the anticipation of joy that gets us through the sorrow. It's the yearning for comfort that makes an uncomfortable situation palatable. One of the things that spurs human growth is the knowledge that foreplay is part of the experience of life. Imagining and anticipating what will come gives the process of growth, of becoming, an enjoyable edge. Unity is great, but growth adds to the experience. If humans are to grow into completeness, they need to shed their skin once in a while.

Look at a picture of yourself as a baby. Then look in a mirror. It may feel like the same you from your position inside of yourself. But no one else sees any similarities.

Your childhood shaped the adult "you." You would not be who you are without those life-changing experiences.

The serpent knew this. You know it. And God knows it. Why else would a good and perfect God have placed the tree of duality, the tree of the knowledge of good and evil, in the Garden if it was not to be used when the time was right? It was a blessing, not a curse. It was only, much later, called a "wicked" temptation by men who did not understand its true nature—men who had fallen under the control of Ego, and used the story to manipulate and control others.

When "Eve ate the apple," we are told, "sin" entered the world.

That is a perverted reading of the myth. The truth was quite different. The knowledge of good and evil, the awareness of duality, spurred the possibility of growth. Humans clothed themselves. To be more accurate, God provided the clothes—the human material body—made of animal skin, the very "stuff" of the creation itself. What a wonderful gift, and proof that the Source is part of the whole process that leads to growth. Humans were once animals, but we are in the process of growing out of it. We never could have done it without divine help.

Primal Soul, consisting of unified male and female energy, thus exited the spiritual garden of wholeness and entered into a material world of atoms and matter—a world of separation—a world of potential—a world of growth. We departed from the Source and became individuals. This individuality, of course, necessitates the birth of Ego. There can be no other way. Individuality begins with an "I." And "I" means Ego.

Did it hurt? Of course! Every birth hurts. Did it bring sorrow? Sure! But without sorrow there can be no discovery of joy. Without pain there can be no experience of health. Growth hurts! It's clumsy. It's uncomfortable. But it is necessary if we are ever to reach wholeness. That's the basic miracle of life. Ideally, pain is to be embraced, not shunned.

Don't be too preoccupied with it. It is not permanent. There is a greater plan in place. Yes, growth hurts. But the pain is not forever. God, you see, has planted another tree in the garden. It's called the Tree of Life. If humans eat from that tree they will live forever.

But who wants to live forever if every day brings growth that involves a constant application of pain, a "shedding" of our skin? So there comes a day when we have grown enough, at least for a while. We call it death. On that day the burden of growth becomes too great to bear. When that time comes, our work of growth is finished. We are permitted to eat the fruit of the tree of life.

As it turns out, we probably have already eaten it. We partook of its fruit back when we lived in the garden. Its potency, however, came wrapped in a time-release capsule. When we finally remember that it already surges through our system, we realize that it was never really forbidden fruit at all. It awaits us upon our return to the garden. It, too, was a blessing, not a curse.

Why does a perpetual life of separation feel so real to those who are living out their lives? Why aren't they aware of all this behind-the-scenes stuff? Why don't humans understand the tremendous journey of growth they are on every day? Wouldn't it make their life easier?

Sure it would. That's what the elders who told the original stories were trying to remind them. But people didn't listen. For the most part, they still don't. They spend most of their lives half-asleep and unaware.

What's the solution? Sleepers, awake! Listen to the story! It involves you. Right now! Just follow the signposts of the elders. They help us to identify the queen, sitting inside, instead of being out in nature where the action is. She is wearily daydreaming of better things. The black window frame contrasts with the white snow. She gazes out the window, separated from life, and sighs. How often have we done the very same thing? Is it any wonder she gets distracted and hurts herself?

As she sewed, she looked up at the snow
and pricked her finger with her needle.
Three drops of blood fell into the snow.
The red on the white looked so beautiful
that she thought to herself,
"If only I had a child as white as snow, as
red as blood, and as black
as the wood in this frame."

So far, the color scheme of our story has been framed only in black and white. Now things change. The color red enters the tale.

Red stands for sacrifice. It is the color of blood. Indeed, we are told that in this case it actually *is* blood. It stains the whiteness of the snow, and things are never again the same.

In the Eden story, when Primal Soul exits the garden of the Source, the place of wholeness, two cherubim are placed on station to guard the entrance. Each holds a flaming sword.

What's the implication? If anyone is to return to the Source, they must first die. We must sacrifice our material bodies in order to return to wholeness. And therein lies the problem. Most of us have come to identify quite strongly with our bodies. The illusion that we *are* our bodies becomes so overpowering that we cannot imagine life without them. We come to believe *The Lie* so strongly that we pour millions of dollars into promoting it. Dying is a tragedy, we say. We must seek ways to live forever. Better to live in a hurting, stinking, illness-prone body than to die.

Oh, we pay lip service to eternal life in the spirit because deep down inside we know physical life will someday end. But when push comes to shove, we'd rather skip the whole death thing.

I once visited a man who was hospitalized after a very severe car crash. His pelvis was crushed and he would never again walk without crutches. His name was placed on a waiting list to receive a kidney transplant when one became available. He was soon going to need a pacemaker. He was hooked up to tubes that monitored his vital signs, fed him intravenously, and provided oxygen to his lungs. He needed hearing aids and wore glasses that looked like bottle caps.

When I bent over his bedside, he slowly recognized me and said words I will never forget: "I guess the Lord wasn't ready for me yet."

What? If ever there was someone ready to exit the body and return to freedom, it was this man. He gave every sign of being a believer in life after death. He faced years of pain and would never return to anything approaching normal life. But he would rather remain in his broken body than give up his faith in *The Lie*.

My father was much the same way. A churchman, and a strong believer in God, he had only one fear. He didn't want to die in a rest home facility. He courageously and unselfishly took care of my mother so she could stay at home and die in bed. But at the age of 98 he faced a decision. He could remain at home, hooked up to oxygen, and receive daily visits from care providers, or submit to a new medical procedure that would involve open-heart surgery. The experimental procedure was only offered at two hospitals in his area. Both were all the way across the state. Both would have been prohibitively expensive were it not for the fact that he had excellent health insurance.

He chose the surgery. After a month in the hospital, it became apparent he would never survive it. At the end he was transferred by ambulance all the way across the state, admitted to a heath care facility near his home, and spent his last days in a hospital bed, drugged up and mostly alone.

As it turned out, he so feared death that he died the death he most feared. To this day, I simply do not understand his decision. I honor it. But I do not understand it.

That's the insidious nature of separation. That's what happens when we believe *The Lie* that we *are* our bodies. We turn into people who sit inside, looking out at life. We become a sacrifice to Ego, the one who believes and perpetuates *The Lie*.

This insight gives us the first real clue about the nature of the queen who sits at the window, looking out at life. Her name is Ego. She views life as if she is looking at a TV screen. She is "in here." Life is "out there." Nature "red in tooth and claw" is not for her. Neither are other people and self-sacrificing situations. In the end, she knows her time is short and doesn't want to be reminded of it.

So she wants to perpetuate herself. She wants an offspring. Not one who will take her place. The queen certainly doesn't want to be deposed. But she knows she can only continue in a body. She will despise anyone who might live forever. Hence, Primal Soul is her sworn enemy. Primal Soul must be kept in check. It is a threatening entity. Ego therefore seeks to remain so self-centered, so loud and boisterous, so active, that Primal Soul cannot get a word in edgewise.

Have you ever sat quietly and tried to find Primal Soul within yourself? It's very difficult. Ego chatters away, doing her best to distract you. Sometimes Primal Soul has to wait for Ego to fall asleep before she can speak at all. When she does, we call it a dream.

A few years ago, when I was just beginning to understand this conflict between Ego and Primal Soul, I had a dream that perfectly explained the situation.

In my dream I was attempting to survey some property I had just acquired. It was a lovely piece of real estate, but when I tried to explore it, I kept getting lost. Obviously, I needed some help. When I looked around to see who might be available, I met an old woman who offered assistance. She was very unpleasant, but she insisted she knew her way around. Eventually she led me into an underground vault of some sort.

The dream began to become frightening. I was extremely claustrophobic. At this point she said to me, "This is where I have to live when you die." She began closing the door behind her. Behind that there was another door ... and another ... and another.

"How do I get out of here?" I asked with some real concern. I noticed colored lines, black and red, painted on the door and corresponding wall.

"It's easy," she said. "Just remember, black on black, and red on red." I had the impression that the colored lines had to match up in order to open the door.

That's when I woke up. Thinking it might be important, I immediately recorded it in my dream journal.

At the time, I was in transition. I had just retired from public life and was living back in the woods of South Carolina. Having spent most of my last 40 years standing in front of groups while lecturing, teaching, and preaching, I was finding it difficult, not having almost daily feedback from people. Although I considered myself a fairly humble man, I was learning that I had come to crave attention and respect. I was one of those people who love to be loved, need to be needed, and want to be wanted. Exiting that kind of addiction cold turkey was proving to be more difficult than expected, especially because I never even suspected I was addicted in the first place.

A fresh way of thinking was just beginning to seep down into my psyche, and I felt this dream might have important ramifications. Our subtle intuition is usually way out in front of our intellectual Ego, so I wondered if I was trying to tell myself something important.

I began to speculate that the new land I was exploring in my dream represented a new dimension of growth that was opening up to me. Perhaps it represented new things I was trying to learn about reality and spiritual truth—the very quest that had led me into the woods to begin with.

It was unfamiliar ground. My rather unpleasant guide seemed to know the way, but instead she led me into a dark place. The woman's name, I have since come to believe, was Ego. She was the queen who sat safely in her room, staring out at the white landscape through a window framed with black ebony, doing something that took up time but was not, at least in the greater scheme of things, very important. That she was vulnerable became apparent when she pricked her finger and began to bleed on the pristine landscape.

The "vault" was my body, the place where Ego lives and rules my days. When I die and return to the beauty and unity of the Source, Ego will die. So she wants me to stay here as long as possible, in the "vault" of my body, because when I'm finished with it and make the journey home, she will die. My sense of separateness will die with her. "This is where I have to live when you die," the old woman said. In that sense, the "vault" was really a grave.

I wonder sometimes if this concept is at the root of what Christian theology calls demon possession. Read allegorically, we *are* demon possessed. The "demon" is Ego, who is threatened whenever we move toward wholeness. Is this "demon" a spiritual entity? Yes! But she is a demon of our own making. She is "fallen" from grace— the grace of Wholeness and Unity. She is doomed to a life of separation.

How do we escape her clutches? She, herself, has shown us the way. "It's easy," she said. "Just remember, black on black, and red on red."

Does the color scheme itself help us at all?

Ted Andrews, in his book *Animal Speak: The Spiritual & Magical Powers of Creatures Great and Small,* may offer up a clue. In a passage about totemic animals, he mentions that Owl and Hawk are often found in tandem. One is a creature of the night, the other of the day. One's color in nature is black, as in night. The other's is red, as in "red tailed hawk." Black is the color of the feminine in nature. It represents earth and dark places such as caves and caverns. Red is masculine. Male birds often display red feathers and features during courting rituals. Red flowers attract humming birds and bees for pollination. Red draws attention to itself. Significantly, it is also the color of blood—the blood of the sacrifice.

Black and red. Night and day. Yin and yang. Masculine and feminine. We return to duality.

The essence of this dream gives us an insight regarding the new colors that have been introduced into the Snow-White story. Red, the color of blood, the color of sacrifice, is now infused into the white landscape. Primal Soul will be born into nature, but she will be born of blood.

The implications of this act are staggering. The cherubim with the flaming swords, posted at the gates of the garden, stand ready to do their job. Before the tale is over, someone is going to die. Will it be Ego or Primal Soul? This is the question that now awaits an answer. The whole point of the story hangs in the balance. Will Ego dominate the world of material creation? Who can contest her supremacy?

Soon afterward she had a little daughter
who was as white as snow,
as red as blood, and as black as ebony
wood,
and therefore, she called her Little Snow-
White.

Now arises a contender for the throne. Ego may be the queen of the material world, but from her blood, Primal Soul takes on material form.

The first stage of historical human development involved Ego adjusting to life in a body. It lasted for millions of years, as we evolved and achieved separation between us and the primates from which we sprang. But then, about 40,000 years ago, and maybe much sooner, something changed. Almost overnight, it would appear, humans developed a higher nature. We began to crawl back into caves deep underground, into the womb of the earth, where we painted magnificent murals on the walls. We developed music. Shamanism was born. We became spiritual beings. We began to look upwards to the heavens, from whence fell the soft snowflakes that set the background for our story.

The stage was now set for an epic duel between Ego and Primal Soul, material existence and spiritual yearning, intellect and intuition. The fate of humankind hung in the balance. Would we return to the earth or ascend to the skies? The story continues to this day.

THE TEXT

The queen was a beautiful woman, but she was proud and arrogant, and she could not stand it if anyone might surpass her in beauty. She had a magic mirror. Every morning she stood before it, looked at herself, and said: "Mirror, mirror, on the wall, who in this land is fairest of all?" To this the mirror answered: "You, my queen, are fairest of all." Then she was satisfied, for she knew that the mirror spoke the truth.

Chapter 2: The Needs of the Ego

The queen was a beautiful woman, but she
was proud and arrogant,
and she could not stand it if anyone might
surpass her in beauty.

Ego can be a beautiful thing. There is nothing wrong with being proud of our accomplishments. The problem lies in becoming arrogant because of them. We strive for perfection, even if we never achieve it. Our reach constantly exceeds our grasp. That's what keeps us moving forward. We want to grow. We want to learn. We want to excel.

What an impoverished world this would be if Claude Monet or Johannes Brahms had said, "That's good enough." There would have been no time-defying, record-breaking, four-minute-mile run if Roger Bannister had said, "4:10? That's pretty fast!" Orville and Wilbur Wright would never have tried to fly. Humans would have looked at the moon and never thought we could go there.

We need a healthy ego. But when our accomplishments dominate our lives, we become arrogant. We don't then *develop* a healthy ego. We *become* Ego. The wicked queen within each of us comes to the surface and takes over. She may look beautiful. But in her pride, she is ugly. Even dangerous.

There is a fine line between ego and arrogance. On one side of that line there is light. On the other, darkness. It is easy to cross over to the dark side. And the surest way to stray into darkness is to become jealous. When *your* success threatens *my* accomplishments, I have begun a downward spiral into spiritual sickness. When I cannot rejoice in your achievement, even in the midst of my failure, I cut myself off from wholeness.

My growth cannot come at your expense. When it does, the evil queen within me takes over my happiness and I suffer for it. I may not realize I am suffering. That is one of the best tricks the evil queen plays. Such is the perversity of Ego that she deceives even her own host.

The world is full of talented people who have wandered into the lair of Ego and fallen under her spell. The fields of sports, politics, science, economics, entertainment, and even religion, are strewn with stories of rise and fall, ego and arrogance. It is one of the greatest tragedies of success that so few learn to navigate its treacherous shoals.

She had a magic mirror. Every morning
she stood before it, looked at herself,
and said: "Mirror, mirror, on the wall, who
in this land is fairest of all?"
To this the mirror answered: "You, my
queen, are fairest of all."

Ego constantly seeks to view itself. "*Every morning*," in fact. But it can see its reflection only in the mirror of its surrounding culture. That is why so many of us need to seek approval from others. They become the mirror in which we view ourselves. We need their praise to validate our accomplishments. It's not enough to do the deed. We want to hear the applause. We want to hear it every day.

"How do I look?" we say. We seldom want to hear the truth. We want affirmation.

"Did you see what I just did?" we ask. Somehow it doesn't seem to count if there are no witnesses.

One of my favorite movie scenes of all times is in the 1993 film, *Indian Summer*, written and directed by Mike Binder. The story takes place at the fictional Camp Tamakwa, a summer camp for kids in Algonquin Provincial Part in Ontario, Canada. A group of alumni, now adults, have been invited back to relive the glory days of their youth, when summers lasted forever, kids fell in love for the first time, and they experienced the exquisite delights and sorrows of transitioning to young adulthood. Not realizing the camp is about to close, they each bring a set of problems with them, not the least of which is the knowledge that, with age, they have all changed.

The Jack Belston character, played by Bill Paxton, was kicked out of camp during his final summer there. Offended by what he understood to be racial bigotry, even at his young age and during a turbulent period of history, he forced his expulsion, moved to California, lived the "Hippy" experience, became addicted to drugs, and became a "Flower Child" of sorts. Now, clean and sober, he has returned to make amends.

But one of the things he learned throughout his life's journey was the danger of Ego. When it came time to participate in the annual "Tamakwathon," a kind of biathlon for kids that involved canoeing and running, he refused. He didn't want to enter into a competition where someone won at the expense of someone else losing.

The next morning, while everyone else slept, he ran the course alone, without witnesses and without a time clock. He ran only for himself, wanting to experience the race without beating someone.

But the wise, retiring camp director, played by Alan Arkin, the one who, years ago, had committed the act of racial bigotry and kicked young Jack Belston out of camp, watched from the shadows, timing him. When it was over, he said, "You would have won, Jack."

But Jack didn't care. Winning was not the point. Running the race and doing his best was enough.

This is a spoiler alert. If you haven't seen the movie yet, you'd better skip this part. But at the end, Jack is the one who takes over the reins from the retiring director. The kid who was kicked out of camp for sticking to his ethical principles and saying "no" to Ego is the adult who takes over and keeps it going in the future.

In the end, Jack discovers that what he had thought was an act of racial bigotry was actually a misguided and long regretted act of cowardly kindness. The camp director had thought he was sparing someone emotional pain and had since lived his whole life with the pain of regret. His confusion produced a mirror-reflection garnered from the expectations and feedback of his culture, not his inward heart. It turns out that both Jack and the camp director had been living in an illusion. Neither one saw an accurate reflection in the mirror of life. Jack's reaction was from the mind. The director's, from his peer group. Sometimes things are not what they seem to be.

Then she was satisfied, for she knew that
the mirror spoke the truth.

A mirror shows only an outward reflection. It cannot reveal inward beauty or purity of thought. As such, it reflects accurately the outward form of whatever is placed before it. But what if that which is placed before it is, in reality, an illusion? Then it will accurately reflect the illusion, rather than the reality.

We live in a world in which we too often view the reflection of illusion, rather than the reflection of truth, so we find it entirely too easy to be deceived. The reason for the deception is Ego. Ego sees only the reflection of itself, and is all too willing to be deceived.

Listen carefully, for instance, to a smiling, bland-faced politician standing in front of a TV camera, speaking, with what passes for utmost sincerity and principle, words that are, in reality, covering up truth rather than declaiming it. It's called political craft. Those who do it best usually get elected.

It's not a new phenomenon. The practice is as old as human Ego.

My home country of the United States is founded upon original principles laid out in a hallowed document called the *Declaration of Independence*. It promises life, liberty, and the pursuit of happiness to each and every one of its citizens. It is a beautiful document, meant to serve as a mirror that reflects the very best of what a government can be. The highest court in the land swears they will defend its sacred words to the full extent of the law, as do all who serve in its shadow.

But think about what the reality mirrored by that document really was, back when it was written.

It offered freedom to all while in reality extending it only to white men of property.

Women, for instance, were not allowed to participate in government. They had to fight for the right to vote. And even now there are vast gender discrepancies when it comes to receiving equal pay for equal work. We have yet to elect a woman president.

Many of the very same men who signed the original document, which offered freedom for all, owned slaves, and considered them to be personal property. It took four score and seven years and a violent and bloody Civil War to fulfill the promises of the Declaration, and another hundred years to officially break through the Jim Crow rules of a bigoted nation. We have yet to make universally true that which was promised more than 200 years ago.

The founders, all either immigrants or children of immigrants, also neglected to include the original inhabitants of the land they now called their own. Any thought of equality for Indians was lost on a trail of tears that eventually led to a place called Wounded Knee.

Unfortunately, the reflection of illusion is not limited to politics. It shines forth whenever Ego rears its ugly head. That means we see it in academia, religion, science, and every other field in which people feel the need to protect a reputation or gather power around themselves.

What all this says is that we have to be careful when we gaze into a mirror. It will show an accurate reflection. But a reflection of what?

The queen saw what she wanted to see. Ego was confident that the mirror spoke the truth. But was that truth couched in reality? Or an illusion? Here's where we need to learn about discernment. We all stand before a mirror and gaze into its depths to visualize our reflection. But what will we see? Who are we, really? And will we accept what we see in the mirror, or will our intention only be satisfied with feedback from other, perhaps less reliable, sources?

It takes great courage to put aside personal fears of inadequacy and confront reality rather than reflection. As we shall soon see, some people just can't do it.

THE TEXT

Snow-White grew up and became ever more beautiful. When she was seven years old, she was as beautiful as the light of day, even more beautiful than the queen herself.

One day when the queen asked her mirror: "Mirror, mirror, on the wall, who in this land is fairest of all?"

It answered: "You, my queen, are fair; it is true. But Snow-White is a thousand times fairer than you."

The queen took fright and turned yellow and green with envy. From that hour on whenever she looked at Snow-White her heart turned over inside her body, so great was her hatred for the girl. The envy and pride grew ever greater, like a weed in her heart, until she had no peace, day and night.

Chapter 3: Confronting Reality

Snow-White grew up and became ever
more beautiful.
When she was seven years old, she was as
beautiful as the light of day,
even more beautiful than the queen herself.

Primal Soul, or intuitive innocence, is a beautiful thing. We see it in children who have not yet learned that life is filled with harsh reality. Sometimes it flashes across the countenance of saints and holy ones. Once in a while we even feel it in ourselves.

In Snow-White, it grew for seven years.

Seven is a sacred number, found in religious texts all over the world. In India we learn of the seven chakras in the human body. Throughout the Bible, every description of God, without exception, is a seven-fold description. The light in the Jewish tabernacle was provided by a seven-stemmed candelabra. And each Sunday morning we are reminded that a new seven-day week lies before us.

The number seven denotes completeness and perfection. Thus it is that at the age of seven, Snow-White is complete and beautiful "*as the light of day*," ready to begin her life's work. Intuitive innocence is full of light and much more beautiful than ego. It springs from within, while ego is developed over time. We are born with innocence. It needs only to flourish. We grow into Ego. It is strengthened every time we seek approval in the mirror of our culture.

One day when the queen asked her mirror:
"Mirror, mirror, on the wall, who in this
land is fairest of all?"
It answered: "You, my queen, are fair; it is
true.
But Snow-White is a thousand times fairer
than you."

There comes a time in every life when the inevitable conflict of Ego and Primal Soul arises. The two collide, sometimes with extreme force.

It's important to remember that at this point in the story, they both inhabit the same house. They live together, Primal Soul having seemingly been born of Ego. But is that really the case? Is there a greater reality at work? Is there a larger picture we need to see?

The truth is that in the story, which up until now has been told largely from Ego's point of view, it appears as though Ego gives birth to primal Soul. But that appearance is an illusion. If Primal Soul is eternal, how can it be preceded by Ego, which is mortal? How can mortality give birth to immortality? It must be the other way around, even though, from Ego's vantage point, Primal Soul is, at this point in the story, only seven years old. What's going on here? Who really came first?

Now is when we need to step outside the picture and pierce the great illusion that exists within the human experience. The truth is, Primal Soul is the creator of the whole human experience. Yes, Snow-White is an actor in the drama. But she is also its author. She has written herself a role within that play. She plays a character who, if the character is to be played honestly, must not be allowed to remember that she wrote the whole play herself.

If that sounds confusing, think of it like this. Imagine that you are a playwright, and you have written a play that explains how you got to be a playwright in the first place. You conjure up the actors, the staging, the props, and the dialogue. You get all the details in writing and then sit back on opening night to watch the curtains rise and the play to begin.

But there's something special about to happen. You have written yourself into the play. The play turns out to be the story of your life, and you play the leading role. So you not only wrote the play, you take part in it. In doing so you do what all good actors do. You completely lose yourself in the part. You *become* the lead character. You forget that you are merely an actor on a stage.

When the play is over you will take your bow and exit the stage. Only then, during the experience which we call death, will you realize that you have participated in a drama starring you. The part you played on stage concerned an actor in a drama. But who was the author of the play?

You were!

What was your name? Snow-White.

Who was the villain of the piece, the one you invented so that you could gain the experiences needed to complete your growth as a human being? The wicked queen, Ego. You needed her as a plot device to make the whole thing work. Because she is a product of your intuitive imagination, she is mortal, designed and created to fulfill an essential role in your growth. Without her, you could not have been born into your creation. She was essential to the story. She needed to give birth to you so you could experience life. But she is mortal. When the play is over and the lights dim, she will cease to exist. Only you, the author, will live on.

You wrote the play and are now living it out. You're such a good actor, and live so totally in character, that you don't realize it. But when the time comes for you to take the final curtain call, you will have arrived back at the beginning of the drama and realize that although the play is now over, it was a resounding success.

Somehow, you know that although Ego is the head villain in your creation, she cannot match up to your essential goodness. Your mind has forgotten all this, but the essential reality known as "You" intuitively knows that you "have" an ego. You are not Ego itself. According to the hallmarks of eternity, ego is a temporary possession of Primal Soul, taken on at birth, developed throughout life, and then discarded at death. Ego is something you have. It is not something you are. It is not in control. You are. Unless you let it take over.

Thus, Primal Soul is "*a thousand times fairer than*" Ego. But Ego can't see through the illusion. As she gazes into her mirror, all she sees is herself. Somewhere, however, beneath the illusion called life-in-the-material-world, she senses her mortality. She senses a presence greater than herself—a god-like presence that is really in control. And it terrifies her.

The queen took fright and turned yellow
and green with envy.
From that hour on whenever she looked at
Snow-White her heart turned over inside
her body, so great was her hatred for the
girl.
The envy and pride grew ever greater, like
a weed in her heart,
until she had no peace, day and night.

When Ego comes to realize she is not in control of her own destiny, that there are mysterious spiritual forces at work in the world, forces too big to really comprehend, she comes to a crossroad. She turns *"yellow and green with envy."* What will her relationship with those forces be?

To put it bluntly, Ego now comes face to face with eternal Spirit. Sometimes Ego is able to let go, take a back seat, and let Spirit rule the roost. But this isn't a story about humility. It's not about sainthood. It's a story about power. Ego doesn't want to retreat into its proper role, live and learn, finish its course and retire, having served its purpose of contributing to spiritual growth. It wants to triumph. It wants a life of its own.

Within the parameters of this particular story, just as within the parameters of many human lives, Ego wants to attain eternal supremacy. When that is allowed to happen, *"envy and pride [grows] ever greater, like a weed in [Ego's] heart, until she [has] no peace, day and night."* If you want to see what this looks like, just look at the world's power-hungry elite who have never learned to say "enough," but always want more. Ego haunts their very faces.

The human race came to this decision point in its evolution at least 40,000 years ago, and probably much earlier. That was the time an early shamanic elite crawled back into the great caves of western Europe and began to draw symbolic paintings on the walls. They drew pictures of images that danced with frightening clarity across the screen of their minds. Spirit was conceived within the human heart. Snow-White was born. It was the birth of religion.

Religion was nothing more than our human attempt to either confront or attune ourselves with the power that lies behind the scenes, above and beyond our comprehension. We called it God. Human Ego sensed that we came from this Source, and will return to this Source, but the illusion of material life was so strong and potent that we could not face the Great Mystery without fear and trembling.

Religion was a human invention designed to alleviate that fear. We hedged ourselves round with doctrines and dogmas. We developed appeasement sacrifices and rituals. Some were as simple as refusing to walk under a ladder or being careful on Friday the 13th. Others were as elaborate as Gregorian Chant and formal prayers sung by a choir.

In all of these practices, individual Ego learned something she still doesn't understand and sometimes cannot accept. She learned that there are forces at work in the cosmos that are more beautiful and greater than she is. She must choose how to deal with them. And on that choice hangs her very fate.

THE TEXT

Then she summoned a huntsman and said to him, "Take Snow-White out into the woods. I never want to see her again. Kill her, and as proof that she is dead bring her lungs and her liver back to me."

The huntsman obeyed and took Snow-White into the woods. He took out his hunting knife and was about to stab it into her innocent heart when she began to cry, saying, "Oh, dear huntsman, let me live. I will run into the wild woods and never come back."

Because she was so beautiful the huntsman took pity on her, and he said, "Run away, you poor child."

He thought, "The wild animals will soon devour you anyway," but still it was as if a stone had fallen from his heart, for he would not have to kill her.

Just then a young boar came running by. He killed it, cut out its lungs and liver, and took them back to the queen as proof of Snow-White's death. The cook had to boil them with salt, and the wicked woman ate them, supposing that she had eaten Snow-White's lungs and liver.

Chapter 4: Out of Eden

Then she summoned a huntsman and said

to him,

"Take Snow-White out into the woods. I

never want to see her again.

Kill her, and as proof that she is dead

bring her lungs and her liver back to me."

So far in the story, we have seen hints that all is not well in Paradise. Ego and Primal Soul have been sharing the same dwelling place, but Ego feels threatened. She is terribly afraid of no longer being #1. At this precise moment she must choose her destiny. If she can act with humility and acceptance, Primal Soul would no doubt reach out both hands in reciprocity and walk together into a hopeful future. But Ego is not a team player. Ego is a necessary part of individuality. You cannot leave the unity of the Source and take on the mantle of individuality without developing an individual ego. That goes without saying. But what part in an individual's life will ego play? Will it choose to blend together with essential Primal Soul, each working toward the common goal of spiritual growth? Or will it demand attention and seek to dominate?

If you want to see this process playing out in your own life, try a little experiment. Sit quietly and try to listen to the voice of your primal soul—your spiritual essence. Try to experience eternal stillness.

You will soon find it is very difficult to do. Your ego will start to chatter away and direct your thoughts to all matter of inconsequential things. It will direct your attention here and there, reminding you of countless things you need to do in the future. It will bring up all sorts of unresolved issues from your past. It will puff up your accomplishments, or, barring that, remind you of your past faults and failures. It will allow you to think of anything and everything except the here and now. In short, it will seek to dominate your thoughts, and thus your life.

Before we became fully modern humans, we lived in the here and now. We were present in the moment. But when we developed a spiritual nature that sought to look beyond the present moment, when Ego was born within us, from the first moments it has sought dominance. With the birth of individual ego, we left the garden of Unity in the Source, the garden of Paradise.

In the mythology of Monotheism, it is called Eden. Two angels, we are told, were placed at the gate of the garden. They were given flaming swords. The implication is clear. In order to return, someone has to die. That someone is Ego. There is no place in Source Unity for Ego, and she is very much aware of the fact that her time is short.

"You kicked me out of the Garden," she shouts, knowing full well that she was never there to begin with and that her birth could only have transpired out here in the material world of individuality.

So, in her anger and futility, she kicks Primal Soul out into the material world of nature, the world she herself is afraid to enter. She is much more comfortable sitting inside, having built a palace of comfort to shield her from the forces of "nature red in tooth and claw." She sits at her window, watching the falling snow, and refuses to go outside where dangers, as well as healing growth, may occur.

That's why when she decides to be the sole queen of her own castle, and condemn Primal Soul to death, she won't do the deed herself. Instead, she gives the job to a huntsman.

Who, therefore, is the huntsman? He is the one who enters into nature, but for the wrong reasons. He loves the woods, but his love is tempered by his own ego. He loves nature, but nature's denizens flee from him. In other words, he loves the natural world for what it will provide him, not for itself. He is not in unity with his environment, although he usually thinks he is. He is an intruder and a predator.

Alas, I know him well. I used to be a huntsman.

Many years ago, I had a friend, now sadly departed from us, whose name was Corser. He was a native New Englander who, probably because he spent time in the merchant marine, tended to call people by their last name. I was always Willis to him, so he is, whenever I think about him, Corser.

To appreciate what he taught me about the identity of the Huntsman we have to travel first on my road, then his. Eventually, as we will see, the two paths will meet and lead us to the insight.

I graduated from the Eastman School of Music in Rochester, New York. At the time I thought I was going to be a full-time professional musician, and for a while I was.

I'm not sure how it happened, me being a budding, big-city music student, but while attending school in downtown Rochester I came under the influence of some men who roamed the woods and fields that, before the building boom of the '70s, made up the countryside outside the city. They had wonderful names. Ben and Ellison, Ken and The Jolly Green Giant, Finley and Cap, all took over where my father had begun 20 years earlier, teaching me to hunt, fish, and play blue grass music.

My way of coping with the city for five weekdays was to have someone drop me off in the woods for the weekend. Equipped only with a hunting knife, knapsack, fishing rod, or rifle, depending on the season, I would live off the land for a few days. If I didn't get anything to eat, I went hungry.

Later, when I took up residence in Massachusetts at the ripe old age of 25 or so, I naturally discovered Corser.

He was in his late 60s then. His hunting partner had just died, a loss any real sportsman will understand, so I gravitated into the vacuum.

Back in those days I measured the success of a hunting or fishing trip by how much game I brought home, since in my early hunting experience, not shooting something meant going hungry. Those days, too, our young family had a tradition that the Thanksgiving table could hold only food I shot, caught, or raised. Vegetables and potatoes from the garden were flanked by a pheasant, a grouse or two, a brace of woodcock on the side, perhaps enhanced by a squirrel, rabbit, or venison roast. The tradition lasted only until my kids got old enough to ask why we couldn't eat turkey like everyone else. But in those days, there were no turkeys in Massachusetts. Never the less, it broke my heart to break the tradition, and to this day, Thanksgiving is not the same.

All this is to say I was a slash-and-burn hunter. When Corser and I went into the woods, I was accompanied by my favorite dog, Corser's two German shorthaired pointers, a shotgun, and an attitude. Dinner depended upon my success. I was under self-imposed pressure. That's the worst kind.

The only advantage the wildlife enjoyed was that Corser didn't want to kill anything, and I couldn't. The spirit was willing, but I was a lousy shot. When all three dogs went on point and a ruffed grouse, or "pat"—that's New Englandeze for partridge—looking at least three feet long, came boiling out of a cover headed for daylight, I sometimes got three shots off into the trees and sky before Corser could yell, "There goes a magnificent specimen of *Bonasa Umbellus*!" He would then apologize to the dogs for not doing his part, and off we would go again.

Corser's road, you see, had been different from mine. He was old enough to remember the glory years of hunting after the war. World War II had kept hunters overseas long enough for farms to grow into bird heaven. Brush piles, overgrown fields and scrub woods, perfect habitat for upland game, had experienced an explosion of birds. They were his glory days, but he had long since outgrown his need to hunt for the table. He was in it now for the dogs and the experience. I never saw him kill a trout. They were always returned to the stream. And on the occasions he did bring down a ruffed grouse for dinner, I always saw a look in his eye that revealed his wish to return the bird back to the cover so he could hunt it again. He enjoyed the *act* of hunting and the *act* of fishing, and he could easily be made to pontificate against those who spoiled the essence of sport.

I will ever be thankful for the insight he passed along to me one morning. I think he had quietly put up with my bird-lust, "Huntsman-ness" until he sensed I was ready for conversion. It was early winter, and we were hunting pats. Corser liked January hunting best. Pheasant season, when we chased those gaudy Korean imports, was closed and the woodcock had all gone south, so we were forced to be purists. Bird hunting meant partridge hunting, and that was as it should be.

All fall he had warned me I was moving too fast, missing the apples that were growing, that year at least, on the ancient trees planted back who-knows-when by old timers who had long since killed their last partridge. Stone cellar holes marked the place where their dreams of forever had come to an end, but lilies-of-the-valley still graced the sites of their old kitchen gardens.

It was a warm day right in the middle of the January thaw, and we had walked back into the woods until we came to a magnificent view of the valley far below. There,

Corser proceeded to sit down on a stump in the middle of an old cut-over and lean his unfired gun against a tree.

I did the same thing.

Eventually the dogs got the idea we weren't doing anything serious that day, so they found a sunny place in a clearing and went to sleep.

I've mostly forgotten what we talked about, but I seem to remember covering a huge amount of philosophical territory. Eventually though, he looked at me and said, "Well, do you suppose we've stayed here long enough so we can go home now?"

I must have looked surprised. "Aren't we going hunting?"

Corser looked at me. "Willis, you've got to understand that sometimes hunting has nothing at all to do with shooting birds!"

A Huntsman is someone who has not yet learned that hunting doesn't necessarily mean killing something. *Our* Huntsman is about to learn this lesson. He has been tasked with killing Snow-White. But because of Ego's natural cowardice, the story here takes a turn.

Our Huntsman may not be operating out of purely spiritual principles, but he at least has love in his soul. He may sometimes be in the forest for the wrong reasons, but he loves the natural world just the same. There is hope in such a person. Corser brought it alive in me. Compassion for Snow-White now brings it alive in the huntsman.

As proof of his dastardly deed, he has been ordered to bring the Queen her victim's liver and lungs. Those are an interesting choice. In Eastern medicine, the liver is responsible for the smooth flow of emotions and blood, as well as the mysterious life energy called "Chi" or "Qi." It is the organ most often associated with excess stress and emotions. The lungs are associated with anxiety.

Stress, emotions, and anxiety are exactly the energy upon which Ego feeds and receives nourishment. Ego doesn't simply want Primal Soul dead. It wants to consume it. It desires nourishment that will keep it alive and growing. It wants to feast on the negative emotional content of what it considers to be forbidden fruit. If it can consume a meal like this, Ego thinks, it will sustain itself forever.

So the huntsman dutifully takes his victim out into nature, little realizing that he himself is about to be changed forever. He is about to awaken a heart of compassion that beats within his breast.

The huntsman obeyed and took Snow-White
into the woods.
He took out his hunting knife and was
about to stab it into her innocent heart
when she began to cry, saying,
"Oh, dear huntsman, let me live.
I will run into the wild woods and never
come back."

Reaching for the knife he has employed to previously kill so much wild game, he starts to stab Snow-White in the heart.

Just as Eastern medicine associates the liver and lungs with definite life energies, the heart is usually associated with joy. The heart is said to "overflow" with love and exuberance. It can be "full" of love. Primal Soul is all heart. So:

Because she was so beautiful the huntsman
took pity on her, and he said,
"Run away, you poor child."
He thought, "The wild animals will soon
devour you anyway,"
but still it was as if a stone had fallen from
his heart,
for he would not have to kill her.

Pity can serve a great purpose. It is usually inspired because of empathy. We feel deeply for someone or something, and take pity on its suffering. We feel them, inside ourselves. We understand their plight. We know what they are feeling because it resonates somewhere deep inside our own being.

"Run away, you poor child," says the huntsman, with compassion and empathy.

But then, because he hasn't yet learned to deal with these foreign feelings, he has to justify his actions. *"The wild animals will soon devour you anyway."* He still feels he has acted out of weakness. But somehow, he knows his actions have magically changed him. He has done the right thing and he knows it, because *"it was as if a stone had fallen from his heart."*

"You old softy," he says to himself. But he knows that, if given the choice, he would do it again. An act of compassion will do that to you, if you let it.

Still, though, he fears the old queen. How is he ever going to explain this away?

Here's where we first receive a hint that something bigger than ourselves is at work in the cosmos, watching over us. Serendipity, sometimes mistakenly called luck, enters the picture. At just that moment, his dilemma is resolved by a power higher than himself.

Just then a young boar came running by.
He killed it, cut out its lungs and liver, and
took them back to the queen as proof of
Snow-White's death.
The cook had to boil them with salt, and
the wicked woman ate them,
supposing that she had eaten Snow-White's
lungs and liver.

Why was it that "*just then a young boar came running by*?" Why not a few minutes before? Why not a few minutes later?

The ancient who first told this story believed that the cosmos was alive and vibrant. If you honor it, and make choices that are good and true, it will come to your aid.

Joseph Campbell was known for many things, but one of them was his famous catch-phrase, "Follow your bliss." He believed that if you honor your true feelings and make decisions based on what is true and important to you, doors will open where before you never thought there were any doors at all.

Carl Jung wrote a whole book about serendipity. There are no accidents when people are following what is near and dear to their heart. Compassion yields a bumper crop of serendipity. We may not see it at the time. It may not always happen in this life. But we can't go wrong when we follow our hearts, for whatever reason. Not in the long run.

In this case, serendipity got our huntsman off the hook. Although it took a lot of salt to make Ego's feast palatable and sweet enough to go down, while she was home, feasting on the lungs and liver of an innocent boar, the huntsman left our story, never to return.

I like to think that he's off in the woods somewhere, leaning back against a tree and watching deer feed off new spring growth. They approach quite close. They somehow know they have nothing to fear.

THE TEXT

The poor child was now all alone in the great forest, and she was so afraid that she just looked at all the leaves on the trees and did not know what to do. Then she began to run. She ran over sharp stones and through thorns, and wild animals jumped at her, but they did her no harm. She ran as far as her feet could carry her, and just as evening was about to fall, she saw a little house and went inside in order to rest.

Inside the house everything was small, but so neat and clean that no one could say otherwise. There was a little table with a white tablecloth and seven little plates, and each plate had a spoon, and there were seven knives and forks and seven mugs as well. Against the wall there were seven little beds, all standing in a row and covered with snow-white sheets.

Because she was so hungry and thirsty Snow-White ate a few vegetables and a little bread from each little plate, and from each mug she drank a drop of wine. Afterward, because she was so tired, she lay down on a bed, but none of them felt right— one was too long, the other too short —until finally, the seventh one was just right. She remained lying in it, entrusted herself to God, and fell asleep.

Chapter 5: Shelter from the Storm

The poor child was now all alone in the
great forest, and she was so afraid that she
just looked at all the leaves on the trees
and did not know what to do.

P rimal Soul now entered the material world. The unity of Eden, in which she was one with all things, had been forsaken. Leaving behind the bliss of eternal Unity, she entered the Great Illusion, was born as a baby into a world she did not understand, and then raised in a household in which she sensed she did not quite belong—a place she knew she could not stay forever. Now she had grown enough to know the truth. She was on her own.

Usually, if we are lucky, the path we follow into the cold, sometimes heartless, world of maturity, involves baby steps. We venture out into the yard, then across the street, then to the houses of friends whose families do things differently than our own, then school, and finally college or jobs. As we learn to navigate the maze and minefield of human relationships, we eventually come to live in our own houses and begin careers that often take us far afield. We grow into adulthood. Ideally, we develop the tools needed to survive and thrive.

Snow-White didn't slowly evolve onto this path. She was violently pushed out, finding herself alone in a great big world that was totally foreign to everything she had up to now experienced. Is it any wonder she "*just looked at all the leaves on the trees and did not know what to do?*"

The material world in which we live can be a frightening place. It is necessary, yes. It is a wonderful school in which to chalk up experiences, learn, and grow. It is a landscape wonderfully designed for consciousness to learn how to examine itself. Eternal and universal Spirit, while enveloped within the unity of the Source, could never learn what it is to be an individual, or undergo the rigorous growth that only being alone can teach. We can never achieve maturity without the pain of separation once in a while.

But it's a scary process, and no one really arrives at full maturity unscathed. Of course, Snow-White was afraid.

We all were, when we made the first, difficult steps along the path to adulthood.

What did she do? She did what we all did. She ran.

Then she began to run. She ran over sharp
stones and through thorns,
and wild animals jumped at her, but they
did her no harm.
She ran as far as her feet could carry her ...

Frantic activity is the hallmark of youth. We run from one experience to another. If you look back at the path of your young life you will surely have vivid memories of *"sharp stones and thorns."* *"Wild animals,"* be they schoolyard bullies, power-hungry adults, supervisors who may have even called themselves teachers, mentors, or priests, unwritten rules that our peer-driven culture insisted upon, poorly defined but accepted customs, and socially accepted norms that made no sense at all, may, in the long run, have done us *"no harm,"* but they certainly left scars. Some of them are so deep that even after we become fully independent adults, we are not aware of how much they have haunted us down through the years.

When I was in elementary school, I was terrified of a kid who, I have recently learned, didn't even remember me. He had been held back in school so he was older and bigger than the rest of us. I don't remember the names of some of my best friends from those days, but I remembered his. I came across his Facebook page and confronted him, long distance, asking if he remembered being a bully. When he responded, saying he didn't recall who I was, for a minute the old terror returned. There is virtually no way in the world that a man well into his seventies could physically threaten me today. But for a moment, the old fear rose up as if it were sixty years ago.

We all have memories of things that might have happened, but didn't—actions that could have had disastrous results which, luckily, didn't transpire, and decisions that, in hindsight, were terrible, but somehow worked out.

There were times, I must confess, that I "*ran as far as [my]feet could carry [me].*" I'll bet you did the same thing.

If we're lucky, though, when we are weary to the bone and can't go any further, we manage to find refuge from what can be a very frightening life.

... and just as evening was about to fall, she
saw a little house
and went inside in order to rest.

We all need shelter from the storm from time to time. It may be found in a job that shows up at just the right time, a person who welcomes us in a warm embrace, a relationship that comes along just when we feel most alone, or a reprieve from an otherwise hopeless situation. But whenever it appears and whatever form it takes, we are able to find physical and emotional relief.

Sometimes our shelter consists of an insight, a sudden way of understanding a riddle about life that had left us concerned and afraid.

A few years ago, for instance, I found myself enduring a time of instability. I had been troubled by epileptic seizures for a few years. To the best of my knowledge, they probably had a psychosomatic basis, brought on by stress. My religion was in the process of slowly being dismantled and broken apart, piece by piece. For a minister, to question that which you had preached and taught your whole life is disconcerting and unsettling, to say the least. The forest of doubt grew thick and close about me.

I had begun to think in terms of vibrational energies that separated alternate dimensions. Epilepsy has been called, since the time of Aristotle, the "Spiritual Sickness" because people who have epileptic seizures sometimes also experience visions and what are usually called hallucinations. Indeed, MRI studies show that what is often called the "shamanic experience," and the OBE experience, affect the same portion of the brain that is lit up during epileptic seizures.

This was also the time I first began to have out-of-body experiences. Somehow, I knew they were related.

After retirement, my wife and I moved to South Carolina with the expressed intention of going on a spiritual retreat. Like Snow-White, I even built a little house in the woods. My goal was to experience the Holy. I had preached about spirituality all my life, but wanted to confront eternal

Spirit. I called it God. My mantra was simple: "I will not let you go until you bless me!" I didn't know how this was all going to work, mind you. But I was fully with the program.

Then I started to have seizures, culminating in an incident in which I got a speck of wood in my eye while doing some chainsaw work. While Barb drove me to an eye doctor, I had the first episodes of what I assume were grand mal seizures—very severe. As they continued during the next year, a few of them were accompanied by impressions of lights, tunnels, and even, one time, people of light standing off to one side.

I did a lot of Internet research and decided I didn't want to take any medications or even see a doctor. My feeling was, strange and egotistical as it may sound, that there was a good possibility that the seizures were happening for a reason. Because I was flirting with out-of-body experiences, which are usually accompanied by a vibrational experience, I felt that they might be opening up a section of my brain that I, through a lifetime of left-brain, academic, theological thought, might have, by habit and misuse, allowed to atrophy.

I'm a pretty rational guy, tending toward scientific and analytical thought. I am also an incurable romantic. For forty years I was a middle-of-the-road, Protestant minister and college professor. I still live most of my waking hours in the left side of my brain, meaning I am normally self-contained to a fault. Religion was a matter of "knowing about" rather than "experiencing."

So when the seizures started at the same time I started seeking a direct relationship with Spirit, I thought it was more than coincidental. I began to think that this was happening for a reason. Were the seizures opening up the very connections in my brain that I would need in order to be responsive to voices from the other side of what I, up to now, had called "reality?" If I chemically closed the door to epileptic seizures, would I also be closing the door to the very spiritual voices I had moved to the woods to discover and encounter?

I began to make some allowances. I didn't drive very much, and I was very careful. But otherwise, I adopted a wait-and-see approach.

Before long I had a vicious seizure that knocked me right off my feet. The immediate neurological results quickly passed. But during the seizure I either broke a bone or two in my foot, or sprained some ligaments and tendons. Six months later the foot was still swollen and tender, probably because I tried to push my recovery too quickly. My other ankle was also quite painful. Walking was very difficult. I was forced to spend many months off my feet, moving only with a cane or walking stick, while wearing ankle braces on both feet.

But that time of inactivity, my shelter from life's emotional storm, proved to be a turning point. I didn't realize it at the time, but the next portion of my life was beginning. I started to take writing seriously. After all, I could write even with one foot up in the air. As a matter of fact, there was very little else I could do.

Since then, I've written many books, numerous magazine articles, and fulfilled a passion I never fully acknowledged I had. I had been running through the woods of life, too "busy" to sit down and discipline myself. I was a teacher who wrote, not a writer who taught. I always wanted to write, and had even written a few books, some of them large and quite imposing. But it was always something I did to "fill in." Somehow, I never felt I had the time. Now I had been forced into a "*little house*" in the woods where I could find rest and security. In that place of inactive safety, an author was born.

> *Inside the house everything was small, but*
> *so neat and clean that no one could say*
> *otherwise. There was a little table with a*
> *white tablecloth and seven little plates, and*
> *each plate had a spoon, and there were*
> *seven knives and forks and seven mugs as*
> *well. Against the wall there were seven*
> *little beds,*
> *all standing in a row and covered with*
> *snow-white sheets.*
> *Because she was so hungry and thirsty*
> *Snow-White ate a few vegetables and a*
> *little bread from each little plate,*
> *and from each mug she drank a drop of*
> *wine.*

Nature, or the real material world, seldom serves up a dinner attended by helpful waiters. It usually offers a buffet wherein we help ourselves. From our point of view, the cosmos, even the little vista we experience, is a huge place, ever expanding outward into infinity. But from the vantage point of an external, non-material, eternal viewer, it is *"small, but so neat and clean that no one could say otherwise."*

Small, but perfectly designed to accomplish exactly that which it was created to accomplish. Everything in the story comes in sevens, the number of completion. The seven-year-old Snow-White finds herself surrounded by seven-fold perfection. She is exactly where she needs to be in order to experience exactly what she needs to experience. She is not living in either the past or the future. She is living in the now, and is thus ready to grow. She has no expectations. She has no memories. She just is.

The wicked Queen Ego wants her dead, the sharp sticks and thorns clawed at her flesh, the wild beasts threatened her. She had every reason to be afraid. The cruel world was spiraling around her in an immense vortex. But here she is safe within the still point of the circle. She has found rest.

There, at that place of safety, the cosmos conspires to meet her needs. A perfect seven-fold feast is laid before her, and she samples a little of everything.

This is, perhaps, one of the most poignant scenes in the whole saga. The old story-teller is reassuring us that when we feel overwhelmed by the swirling vicissitudes of life, we need to find the still point at the center of our being. Everyone looking in from the outside may offer us advice—do this, do that, do the other thing. Life is full of critics. But their so-called solutions always seem to involve "doing" something.

The ancients, even though they lived in a much quieter time than those of us who dwell in the hectic 21st century, foresaw the inevitable. Here, they warn us that when life swirls around us in an endless, revolving cyclone, we can find safety not by doing but by being. In the eye of the storm, the cosmos will place before us a perfect feast that will meet our needs of the moment.

And unknown Jewish song writer from long ago said it clearly and succinctly: "You prepare a table before me in the presence of mine enemies. My cup runneth over."

Good advice, for a hectic age!

*Afterward, because she was so tired, she
lay down on a bed,*

but none of them felt right—one was too
long, the other too short—until finally, the
seventh one was just right.

In our journey through life, some beds are always going to be too long. Some will always be too short. The trick is to find the one that best fits us at our present place of growth.

The natural human tendency is always to identify with that which is good, comfortable, or otherwise desirable. When we find the metaphorical bed that fits us best, we call it "good." If it is too long or too short, we call it "bad." Whole religions have been designed to teach us to identify with that which is "good" and reject that which is "bad."

But who are we to judge? How can we possibly know the ins and outs of what is good and bad?

Picture a beautiful spring scene in your mind. The sky is a deep blue with a few white, puffy clouds hanging quietly beneath a brilliant sun. The grass has turned a bright green, and robins hop joyfully upon its surface. Trees are starting to leaf out, and the promise of summer lies over all.

It's a beautiful picture, isn't it? But back up to those robins for a minute. What are they doing on that bucolic lawn? They're eating worms! Great sport, if you're a robin. But what about the worm? Your beautiful red-breasted ambassador of spring could equally be a feathered monster from on high. It all depends on your perspective.

How can we really know, in every case, what is good and what is bad? Sometimes it's simply impossible. Even while we are safe in the still point of our circle, with life swirling around us in a vortex of danger, some beds will always be too long, and some beds will always be too short. This does not make them "bad." Sometimes things are much too complicated for our small minds. Let the universe handle the details. The trick is to find the resting place that best fits your present stage of growth. Find your safe place. Lie down in it and relax. Don't fight life. Let it come to you.

She remained lying in it, entrusted herself
to God, and fell asleep.

An old friend of mine, recognizing my hard-driving tendencies, used to remind me from time to time, "If at first you don't succeed, stop and take a nap."

Good advice, indeed.

THE TEXT

After dark the masters of the house returned home. They were the seven dwarfs who picked and dug for ore in the mountains. They lit their seven candles, and as soon as it was light in their house, they saw that someone had been there, for not everything was in the same order as they had left it.

The first one said, "Who has been sitting in my chair?"

The second one, "Who has been eating from my plate?"

The third one, "Who has been eating my bread?"

The fourth one, "Who has been eating my vegetables?"

The fifth one, "Who has been sticking with my fork?"

The sixth one, "Who has been cutting with my knife?"

The seventh one, "Who has been drinking from my mug?"

Then the first one saw that there was a little imprint in his bed, and said, "Who slept on my bed?"

The others came running up and shouted, "Someone has been lying in mine as well."

But the seventh one, looking at his bed, found Snow-White lying there asleep. The seven dwarfs all came running up, and they cried out with amazement. They fetched their seven candles and shone the light on Snow-White. "Oh, good heaven! Oh, good heaven!" they cried. "This child is so beautiful!"

They were so happy, that they did not wake her up, but let her continue to sleep there in the bed. The seventh dwarf had to sleep with his companions, one hour with each one, and then the night was done.

Chapter 6: Keepers of the Sacred Flame

*After dark the masters of the house
returned home. They were the seven
dwarfs, who picked and dug for ore in the
mountains. They lit their seven candles,
and as soon as it was light in their house,
they saw that someone had been there,
for not everything was in the same order as
they had left it.
The first one said, "Who has been sitting in
my chair?"
The second one, "Who has been eating
from my plate?"
The third one, "Who has been eating my
bread?"
The fourth one, "Who has been eating my
vegetables?"
The fifth one, "Who has been sticking with
my fork?"
The sixth one, "Who has been cutting with
my knife?"*

The seventh one, "Who has been drinking
from my mug?"
Then the first one saw a that there was a
little imprint in his bed, and said,
"Who slept on my bed?"
The others came running up and shouted,
"Someone has been lying in mine as well."

We now meet some new characters in the drama, and once again the number seven permeates the narrative. The seven dwarfs have been so Disneyfied that anyone who has seen the classic cartoon version of the movie finds it both difficult and disappointing to learn that in the original version of the story, they are neither named nor described. They don't even sing. Never the less, they serve an important role in moving the plot forward.

Once again Snow-White is befriended by those with close ties to nature. First it was the Huntsman. In this case, the seven dwarves, who made their living by delving deep into nature's secrets and extracting her precious treasures. They "*picked and dug for ore in the mountains.*"

There are two ways to live in and with nature.

The first is that of the locust. Locusts devour everything in their path. They destroy and then move on. In doing so, they doom their own existence, but such is their ferocity, and need for immediate gratification, that they don't seem to care. More and more these days, it seems as if most of the human race resembles locusts. We are a destructive species whose ego is bent on personal hunger and greed.

But there is another way to interact with nature. That is the way of the bee. Bees take what they need while giving back at least as much as they receive. They pollinate and nurture, causing nature to reproduce itself, grow, and flourish. They store that which they take, and produce sweet honey in return. Nature would be at a great loss without bees. Neither could flourish without the other. Here's hoping the human race soon begins to emulate bees rather than locusts!

The seven dwarfs fall somewhere in the middle. Much like the Huntsman, their hearts are obviously in the right place. But unlike bees, there is little evidence that they return to nature a bounty equal in value to that which they pry from her. So once again we are faced with people who value nature for her abundance, but don't quite live in perfect symbiosis with her. They live in *nature*, but not in *Eden*. In that, they are just like us.

But they do serve an important purpose. When Snow-White is alone in the darkness, they prove to be keepers of the sacred flame. When they light their seven candles, illustrating again the perfection of the light they guard, they reveal the beauty of Primal Soul, asleep and unaware of their presence.

Sometimes it may feel as though we are alone in the darkness, but a benevolent cosmos is watching over us as we sleep in the darkness of the Great Illusion called material existence. The Keepers of the Flame recognize that we are intruders, simply passing through in our journey from life to death. But they recognize the importance of those who are the individual personification of eternal consciousness involved in the process of learning the ways of finite existence.

But the seventh one, looking at his bed,
found Snow-White lying there asleep.

The seven dwarfs all came running up, and
they cried out with amazement.
They fetched their seven candles and shone
the light on Snow-White.
"Oh, good heaven! Oh, good heaven!" they
cried. "This child is so beautiful!"

To those who live their lives surrounded by nature, but not really one with her—to those who have been cast out of Eden without really losing their innate appreciation of Eden's attributes—it is refreshing to come across innocent beauty. It is surprising, even, to meet those who are untouched by the meanness and pettiness so often found in "worldly" people. The true and real home of Intuitive Innocence is recognized. It is not of earth. *"Oh, good heaven! Oh, good heaven!" they cried.* They knew where the source of Primal Soul really abides.

Maybe it's for this reason that people who demonstrate intuitive innocence are sometimes suspected of harboring hidden agendas. "They can't really be that naive," we say. And even when their innocence is proven beyond a shadow of a doubt, we may admire it, but consider it beneath our level of sophistication. True innocence just doesn't seem to belong down here among humans. No, we admire guile. We respect cleverness. But we sometimes recognize honest innocence when we see it. Maybe that's why we like dogs so much. They are utterly without guile.

I once was moved to write a story about two people who decided to live an authentic life, free from guile. I speculated that perhaps the cosmos might even reward such people. I'm going to take a short break from our narrative and share it now, because it is important to be reminded of the benefits of honesty in the midst of a dishonest world.

Timothy's Story:

A Fantasy for Troubled Times

At exactly 2:17 PM, on May 12th, Timothy Philbrick quit his job.

He hadn't planned to do it. When he left for work that morning, after having breakfast with his wife and saying goodbye to the kids, he had picked up his backpack/briefcase, fired up the Nissan and headed out onto the highway for his regular forty-five-minute commute. It was unseasonably warm. The birds were singing, and there was springtime softness in the air that carried a hint of summer in it. Grass was greening up, so the first lawnmowers of the year had hatched with a roar and a whine.

Business as usual.

He had stopped for coffee at his customary haunt, said the required niceties to the regulars, and entered his cubicle at exactly 7:59 AM. The morning number crunches went well, and by noon he was right on schedule.

The problem began when he went outside to eat lunch on the lawn behind his building. Sitting quietly on one of the benches, placed strategically under one of the six scraggly trees (he counted them every day), he realized that he should have been happy, but wasn't. He had a decent job. It wasn't challenging, but it paid average money. They were getting by, what with the small income his wife brought home. Their mortgage was under control. The car payments were manageable. They didn't quite have a month's income in the bank, but as long as they didn't think about what college would someday cost for their teenager, they figured they were as well off as the other families on the block.

He didn't know why, but somehow, he just couldn't stand the thought of going back into that cubicle to face his computer screen.

The one o'clock chime from the church belfry across the street stirred him to consciousness, but his heart wasn't in it. He punched keys and crunched figures until 2:04, then just stopped and stared into space. He couldn't explain what was happening to him, but he suddenly felt he had come to a crossroad — that what he decided right now would determine his eternal destiny. It sounded melodramatic, but there it was. The world had stopped revolving, and the future of everything he believed in somehow hung in the balance. Ten minutes passed but he was not aware of a single sound, a single movement. It was strange. He experienced a profound stillness even though there was a small part of his consciousness that imagined the screaming voices of his family, his friends, and even his long dead father.

"What are you doing?" they cried. "You are a responsible adult! People depend on you! Get back to work. Earn your paycheck!"

But he just sat there until 2:17. Funny. He noticed the time and remembered it, cataloguing it away as if for posterity. Then, slowly, as if an outside force had taken over his body, he got up, walked over to the glass door that protected Alicia, his supervisor, from riff-raff such as himself, opened it, and simply walked in. He didn't knock. He didn't wait to be invited. He just entered the office that he hadn't been in since he was hired twelve years ago.

Alicia looked up at him with a distracted expression, her desk littered with papers and stacks of forms.

"What do you want?" she asked.

"Nothing," Tim replied. "It's just that I have to get out of here. Right now. I can't do this anymore. I'm turning in my notice."

She didn't say a word. She just

looked at him, her face a mask of incredulity.

"What are you going to do?" she asked.

"First, I'm going to go somewhere and get a good, stiff drink. After that, I don't have the foggiest notion."

Another silence. She just stared at him.

"Just like that? You're leaving just like that? And you don't have another job or any idea how you're going to get by?"

"Sounds crazy, doesn't it? But, yeah. Just like that. If I go back to that cubicle I'll die right now, and spend the rest of my life waiting for my body to catch up. That's it. I'm leaving."

Yet more silence. This time it dragged on forever. Alicia just stared at him.

Finally, she spoke, her voice tense and cracked with emotion. "Wait a minute," she said. "I'm coming with you."

Now it was Timothy's turn to stare. "Don't you understand? I'm leaving the company. I'm quitting. I won't be back. You can't talk me out of it. This is something I have to do."

"I know," she said. "Me too." And she picked up her purse, grabbed her light sweater, and headed out the door.

Life on the cube farm continued as if the earth hadn't stopped spinning. Nobody noticed that the world had just changed unalterably. In fact, nobody noticed anything. Like "Ol' Man River," they just kept rolling along.

Tim and Alicia rode the elevator down to the first floor in a silence so loud it was deafening. As they walked through the lobby Tim almost started to giggle when he got the absurd idea that somehow a security officer was going to arrest him and send him to the principal's office. He was almost giddy with the freedom he felt. He was scared. Petrified, in fact. Ignored voices of reason began to scream in his turned-off but still present brain: "What do you think you're doing? You can't just quit your job. Isn't there a law about that or something?" He felt like a little kid about to get caught. And he felt like a grown-up adult, free on the earth, for the first time in his life. Part of him wanted to run and shout and do cartwheels in the springtime. And part of him wanted to quietly go back to his cubicle and hope no one had noticed anything.

But there was Alicia, his supervisor, standing right next to him, no doubt feeling the same thing. Only she wasn't his supervisor anymore. She was just another human being, like himself. And what was she thinking? She hadn't said anything. Had he just assumed she felt what he was feeling? God! He didn't know anything about her. Why had she come with him? What was he doing? What were they doing?

What was going on?

By 2:38 they were ensconced in a little bar across the street. By 3:47 they were old friends. By 5:05, when he called home to tell his wife he would be late, they were business partners. They had agreed they could make a difference in the world by utilizing her business sense and his technical expertise. They had even laid down some hard and fast rules:

First—no dehumanizing cubicles. The queen bee and the drones would all work in the same flower patch.

Second—they would share the wealth. Some would cultivate and some would pick weeds but, since both chores were needed to produce a crop, the gardeners would all eat the same amount of vegetables when harvest time arrived.

Third—honor system. They would hire a team, not employees. Once a worker proved trustworthy, she wouldn't need to explain why she had to skip a day or be late to work. Why should some supervisor make the decision whether a kid was sick enough to warrant a parent staying home?

Fourth—well, there was no fourth. That's as far as they got. But they felt pretty confident that the rest would follow.

It wasn't easy, going home that night. Tim had to explain why he had quit his job and spent the afternoon drinking with his former supervisor, a woman his wife had never met. He had to face questions for which he simply had no answers. His family didn't understand. Tim didn't blame them. He didn't understand either. There were tears and accusations. He felt unbearably guilty at times.

But he had never been happier in his whole life.

* * *

Thirty years, one month and four days later, Dr. Timothy Philbrick sat on the dais at the graduation exercises of State University, prepared to give yet another commencement address. He never tired of it. The preliminaries got a little boring, but no matter, it gave him a chance to reminisce.

Thirty years! Sometimes he couldn't believe it. Where had the time gone? The company pretty much ran itself now. His son was CEO and, by every report, doing a bang-up job. Alicia was semi-retired and up in Seattle, doing pro bono work for some conservation group. His other kids were successful in different fields, but doing well and instilling in other businesses the same principles he had built into his own. It had been a satisfying and happy time. He wasn't rich by any means. But that didn't matter. It never had.

The first few years had been

difficult, requiring long hours and some scary financial decisions, but he and Alicia had stuck to their guns. They never hired employees. They formed a team. And what a team it was! Oh, sure, a few times someone had taken advantage of them. But for the most part the people who worked with them appreciated the work ethic and atmosphere so much that they stayed their entire careers. There were even a few youngsters working with them who were the grandchildren of the original team members.

He had to laugh at that. Following their first rule, he and Alicia had worked in the same room and under the same conditions as everyone else in the company. That had caused rampant speculation when the corporation grew enough to require expanding into new office space. They had moved into the second floor of a complex located on the outskirts of town. Alicia had insisted on looking at lawns and trees, not a lot of traffic. The only problem was that the second floor of their new corporate digs sported a rather large corner office with a splendid view. The team was waiting to see who would get it. Constitutionally, Alicia was CEO. But Tim was tech engineer. More than a few good-natured, but private, bets were wagered. In the end, everyone lost. Neither Tim nor Alicia would take the office. It served as a storage room for a few months, until one of the team members had an idea that was unanimously approved at the next monthly team meeting. The company hired a specialist in early childhood development, and turned the corner office into a nursery for young children of team members. Once in a while it caused a little confusion when a toddler got loose and wondered into the main office. After all, the kids could see mom or dad working right on the other side of the glass doors. Aside from that, everyone loved the setup, although there was a tendency to get into good natured arguments about who got to take babysitting breaks. A few of the kids who had grown up considering the office nursery their second home now worked there as part of the team.

Experienced team members had no problem adjusting to the working conditions. In some cases, they had never known anything else. But new employees were sometimes taken aback. Tim fondly remembered the surprise on the face of a recently hired computer tech who hadn't quite finished a project when quitting time came one day. He asked if he could stay for another hour.

"Sure," Tim had replied, and given the man his keys. "Lock up when you're done." The guy had been flabbergasted.

"You mean—you're going to trust me with the keys to the place? Just like that?"

"Well, actually, no," Alicia had chimed in. "Tim, I'm going to be late tomorrow so you'll have to open up."

Turning to the tech she said, "Here, take mine instead." And she gave him her keys to the building. "I'll pick them up tomorrow when I get in."

The guy still worked with the company, fourteen years later. He even brought his newborn son to the nursery sometimes. He didn't need to. His wife was a stay-at-home mom, but he did it just because he wanted his colleagues to meet his family.

What finally landed the company on the cover of both *Newsweek* and *Forbes* was that after things had settled down a bit, and operations had pretty much smoothed out, Tim decided he wanted to go back to school. Following their corporate style of accountability, he had first brought the matter up at a monthly team meeting. Outsiders couldn't figure out why Tim had to ask permission from his employees to do something like that, but Tim and Alicia hadn't seen it that way at all. They were a family. A corporate family, to be sure, but a family just the same. So Tim, realizing he wasn't going to be able to shoulder what he considered a fair burden of work, offered to take a pay cut for the duration of his time in school.

The rest of the team wouldn't hear of it. In fact, they voted a share of corporate profits to pay for Tim's tuition, with the stipulation that he would share with them what he was learning in his studies. He had gone on to earn an advanced degree in world religions, offering stripped-down seminars during company time for any who wanted to attend. The discussions and helpful insights these sessions prompted had been more than worth it to the team members. They felt they were going to college while working.

With their encouragement, Tim had gone on to earn a doctorate in cross-cultural spirituality. But paying for Tim's schooling prompted another popular company policy. Children of team members had their college tuition paid for. It was as simple as that.

When asked by a reporter how the company could afford it, Tim had grinned over at Alicia and said, "Easy. Our CEO works dirt-cheap!" That statement, when quoted prominently in *USA Today*, echoed through the corridors of many a board room.

They knew they had finally arrived when they were approached by the Board of Directors of their former company, the one Tim and Alicia had walked out on that spring afternoon so long ago. With their business attracting more than regional acclamation, Alicia had been offered a huge incentive to cash in and sell out. They attended the meeting out of curiosity, but never really expected to close a deal. So Tim tried hard to keep a straight face when Alicia was encouraged to retire.

"At your age," they said, "you've got to consider your bottom line."

"What are you talking about — 'age'

and 'bottom line'?" she had replied. "Are you telling me I'm old and fat?"

At that point, Tim lost it. He was laughing so much he had to leave the room and the meeting was pretty much over.

Other companies saw what was happening. They respected results and they recognized corporate success. More and more, Tim was asked to speak at national corporate meetings in many different industries. Over and over again he told his story, preaching the gospel he called the spiritual principles of corporate success. In the process he had a tremendous effect on the market place. Companies slowly came to the conclusion that they had to treat their employees with dignity, respect, and trust if they wanted to attract the best and brightest. The *Today Show*, capitalizing on his religion degree, introduced him as the "Motivational Maharishi."

Alicia didn't let it go to his head,

though. She started calling him "Yogi." "Hey Yogi, get your face out of your press clippings and get over here. I need help with this!" Much to Tim's chagrin, the name stuck. But secretly, he kind of liked it.

Thinking back over thirty years, lost in a brief reverie, Tim was surprised when he suddenly heard his name.

"State University is proud to welcome to the lectern our commencement speaker, Dr. Timothy Philbrick."

As had happened so many times before, Tim was overwhelmed by the response, and nervous as well. He never believed he had anything special to say. His message was always different in terms of illustrations and local particulars, but it remained basically the same. It was simple, really. People needed to put away thoughts of power and control and celebrate the miracle of what it is to be human. That's all there was to it.

The applause died down, and he began to speak ...

Back to Snow-White

The point of this story is that the cosmos will, sooner or later, reward people who are free from guile, who are the personification of Intuitive Innocence, who follow their heart and Primal Soul rather than their scheming minds. Of such is the kingdom of heaven. The seven dwarfs may not have demonstrated Primal Soul completely in their own lives, but they recognized it when they saw it. And they honored it so much that they were even willing to suffer a little discomfort to protect it and keep it safe and comfortable.

They were so happy, that they did not wake
her up, but let her continue to sleep there
in the bed. The seventh dwarf had to sleep
with his companions,
one hour with each one, and then the night
was done.

137

THE TEXT

The next morning Snow-White woke up, and when she saw the seven dwarfs, she was frightened. But they were friendly and asked, "What is your name?"

"My name is Snow-White," she answered.

"How did you find your way to our house?" the dwarfs asked further.

Then she told them that the queen had tried to kill her, that the huntsman had spared her life, and that she had run the entire day, finally coming to their house.

The dwarfs said, "If you will keep house for us, and cook, make beds, wash, sew, and knit, and keep everything clean and orderly, then you can stay with us, and you shall have everything that you want."

"Yes," said Snow-White, "with all my heart."

So she kept house for them. Every morning they went into the mountains looking for ore and gold, and in the evening when they came back home their meal had to be ready. During the day the girl was alone.

The good dwarfs warned her, saying, "Be careful about the queen. She will soon know that you are here. Do not let anyone in.

Chapter 7: Rise of the Patriarchy

The next morning Snow-White woke up,
and when she saw the seven dwarfs
she was frightened. But they were friendly
and asked, "What is your name?"
"My name is Snow-White," she answered.
"How did you find your way to our house?"
the dwarfs asked further.
Then she told them that the queen had tried
to kill her,
that the huntsman had spared her life, and
that she had run the entire day,
finally coming to their house.

It can be a frightening thing to suddenly confront the natural world for the first time. Everything seems bigger, more menacing, even threatening. A small scurrying in the leaves sounds like the footsteps of a fierce beast when you're all alone in the darkness. It takes a while to realize that just because something or someone is different, maybe even scary, it doesn't necessarily mean they mean you any harm. When Snow-White awoke from her sleep, she was about to begin a new phase of life in an unfamiliar environment. Like all such transitions, it began with fear and trembling. "*When she saw the seven dwarfs, she was frightened.*"

Colin Fletcher, before his untimely death, was known as the official grand-daddy of backpackers everywhere. He was the author of the book *The Complete Walker. Field and Stream* magazine dubbed it "the hiker's Bible." Over the years, it was revised four times. His first book, *The Thousand Mile Summer*, was also a best seller. That's the book that first led me to write to him. We corresponded a few times over the years. I often call him "a mentor whom I've never met."

At the outset of his trek from Mexico to Oregon, up the east side of California, the long walk that catapulted him into fame, he was a self-confessed novice when it came to backpacking. He was also relatively new to California, being British by birth, and completely new to the desert. So it's understandable that when he faced down his first rattlesnake, he killed it in a fit of terror. Likewise, the second and third. By the time he met his fourth, he began to be less afraid and more curious. He started watching and learning, rather than reacting. Eventually he wrote a definitive article about the American Rattler for *Family Safety* magazine. It demonstrated real growth on his part, from the initial fear of confrontation, through grudging acceptance, to something bordering on affection.

Snow-White passed through these same stages when she first met those Keepers of the Sacred Flame who would make possible her growth in the natural world. She went from fear to completely trusting her new-found friends, eventually sharing her whole story. Her safe place had begun to feel like a new home.

We often experience the same feelings when we first confront spiritual serendipity in the guise of real people. They are the Keepers of the Sacred Flame, who, usually without knowing they are doing so, say or do just the right thing at the right time—just what we needed to hear when we needed to hear it. Sometimes a long dead author leaves us a message in a book that might sit unread on our shelves for years. Then, when we need it most, a paragraph jumps out and provides the wisdom we need at a particular moment in our lives when we are ready to accept it. The sacred flame burns constantly, ready to light our way through the darkness. It offers safety in the chaos of life.

In Snow-White's case, unfortunately, that safety came with a price.

The dwarfs said, "If you will keep house for us, and cook, make beds, wash, sew, and knit, and keep everything clean and orderly,
then you can stay with us, and you shall have everything that you want."
"Yes," said Snow-White, "with all my heart."
So she kept house for them. Every morning they went into the mountains looking for ore and gold, and in the evening when they came back home
their meal had to be ready.
During the day the girl was alone.

The story takes quite a turn at this point. Yes, Primal Soul was now relatively safe and secure, protected and cared for by the seven dwarfs. But there was a price to pay for her security. While the "men" went off to work, the "little woman" was left behind, doing what has often been described as "woman's work."

When I first heard that term, it came from the lips of an eight-year-old boy. We teach the concept of patriarchy, of men's dominance over women, right from the cradle, it would seem, even when we are not aware we are doing it.

No one knows, for sure, when the practice began. The first signs of it in the archeological record go back as far as the Neolithic Era—the "New Stone Age"—the age of the Agricultural Revolution. 12,000 years ago, and almost certainly a long, long time before that, it appears, with a few notable exceptions, that most men, in most cultures, were primarily hunters. Women did most of the gathering of natural plants, eventually learning how to grow their own. By then, humans had figured out that it took both a male and a female to produce offspring. As luck would have it, it was also the time people began to take over private ownership of individual flocks and herds of newly domesticated livestock. During the Paleolithic Era, land and supplies had been shared in common by the whole tribe. But in the Neolithic, things changed. Private ownership of both land and herds began. It also led to the birth of what we call civilization, which produced the building of cities, specialized labor, the art of writing, and a whole lot more.

Together, all these elements swirled into a perfect storm. Patriarchy was institutionalized as a central pillar of what was to become a world-wide civilization. "This is mine" and "that is yours." Men were in charge and women were relegated to child rearing and keeping the home fires burning. It was a culture perfect for the growth of Ego and hording. "I want to keep it so I can pass it down to my offspring."

Speaking of offspring, it soon became apparent to men that they wanted unquestioned ownership of their children as well. The wanted to be the undisputed head of the house. Unlike men, women needed to remain virgins until marriage, so there could be no doubt of who the father was. The concept of the undisputed heir became paramount. Any child born out of wedlock was a bastard, a pejorative term that reflected on both the innocent child and his mother, but seldom on the man involved. Right up to the time of the Scarlet Letter of Puritan fame, and even to this day in many parts of the world, both having a baby "outside of wedlock" and the act of adultery is punished, sometimes by death.

It wasn't long before women began to be seen as commodities. Arranged marriages were only one example of this practice. Children became an economic asset. From there it was only a short step to misogyny. A woman's place was in the home, having children, and taking care of the house.

Thus it was that Snow-White's protection and care came with a price tag. "*If you will keep house for us, and cook, make beds, wash, sew, and knit, and keep everything clean and orderly, then you can stay with us, and you shall have everything that you want.*"

By the time this story was first told long ago, patriarchy was already seen as the accepted and normal way for society to function. It would have been nice if Snow-White had other choices. But given her culture's norms, there wasn't much else she could do. "*Yes,*" she said, "*with all my heart.*"

If this were simply a story about patriarchy, about a social system in which men hold power and exclude women from attaining important positions of leadership and personal fulfillment, we could stop right here and acknowledge that this is already a powerful saga. There is something heartbreaking about Snow-White, like uncounted millions of women before her, being forced into a position of servitude just to be able to survive.

But the ancient author's intent was not to just expose patriarchy as a social evil. He was using it as a metaphor to describe something even more sinister. He is telling us that throughout history, men's dominance over women is analogous to our dominate culture's attitude toward Primal Soul—toward Intuitive Innocence. We value it. We put it on a pedestal. We laud it, and wish there were more examples of it in public life. But at the core of our being, we consider Primal Soul—Intuitive Innocence—to be naive and weak. It's too easily pushed around. We applaud it at the same time we consider it too frail to be of practical importance in the arena of power.

The innocent person gets shoved around and bullied. Deep down in our hearts, we don't respect them. We want Innocence to stay in its proper place, not out in the rough and tumble world of day-to-day reality.

Whatever your political position may be, there was a great truth revealed once in an interview held with Tip O'Neill, the long-time Speaker of the House of Representatives. The interviewer asked O'Neill what he thought of President Jimmy Carter, after Carter had left office after only one term. It was no secret that the two had their differences, despite the fact they were both Democrats.

O'Neill was a veteran of the tough, Irish, Boston political machine. He grew to become a Washington insider, through and through. It was often said of him that "he knew how to get things done!"

Carter was a southern Sunday School teacher—a farmer from the little town of Plains, Georgia. He was a Washington outsider whose experience as governor of a southern state was seen as less than qualifying for the brutal insider politics of our nation's capital.

O'Neill knew how to apply political pressure, make deals, and wrestle his agenda through the ranks. Carter was a man of principle who, though a Democrat, thought of himself first and foremost as a representative of all the people.

Maybe that's why O'Neill, when asked about how history would view the Carter presidency, said that Jimmy Carter was too good and decent a man to be president.

Perhaps that explains the position too many people take when it comes to leadership. We pay lip service to Intuitive Innocence and spirituality, but think ego-centered strongmen are the only ones fit to lead. Primal Soul's place is back home, doing the things needed to make life more comfortable for the real leaders of the world.

Primal Soul does no better in the arena of our day-to-day lives. Somewhere, down deep in our hearts, our souls take a backseat to our egos.

"You know meditation is important. Do you meditate every day?"

"I don't have time. My work keeps me too busy."

"Spiritual growth is important. Do you nurture it in yourself?"

"Well, I try to treat people as I would want to be treated. But that doesn't always work."

"Don't you realize people are out to get you?"

"I try to look for the good in everyone, no matter how rotten they are. But, yeah, you can't really trust people."

On and on it goes. We admire holiness in others. But we don't take the time to nourish it in ourselves.

The seven dwarfs symbolize a well-meaning society that respects nature enough to appreciate its bounty, but takes without giving back, not recognizing that it was Mother Earth who first gave us birth and continuously offers spiritual enrichment if we only open our eyes and hearts. It appreciates the beauty of Intuitive Innocence, but keeps it home, under wraps and out of sight, where it belongs. Society is not necessarily made up of bad people. The dwarfs were certainly helpful when it came to protecting Snow-White. But they operated in what they considered to be the "real" world, where they assumed she had no place.

They personify the cry of a patriarchal culture: "I love the little woman! She's too important to soil her hands out in the world. Better she stays home and minds the house, keeping the home fires burning, cooking, cleaning, and making my life easier! Why should she have to worry her pretty little head?" Thus, we idealize our false conception of innocent beauty, while keeping it safely out of life's arena.

All the while, the patriarchal institution is so ingrained in our culture, and has been for so long, that many people actually come to think it's somehow God-ordained and the way things are supposed to be.

> *The good dwarfs warned her, saying, "Be*
> *careful about the queen.*
> *She will soon know that you are here. Do*
> *not let anyone in."*

This raises an interesting question. The dwarfs had a good thing going. They were much better off than before. Now, when they got home, a hot meal was waiting on the table. Perhaps we are being unkindly suspicious, but when they warned Snow-White to watch out for her nemesis, the queen, did they have only her best interest at heart, or did they also want to protect the status quo?

It's an interesting thought. But that's the way things usually are out in the material world in which we live.

Motives are always a little mixed. We find ourselves justifying actions that we swear spring from pure intentions, while ignoring the fact that we, ourselves, can't always trust our own words.

"Know thyself," said Socrates, quoting the Oracle of Delphi. Shakespeare said it a little differently: "To thine own self be true, for it must follow as dost the night the day, that thou canst not then be false to any man."

Good words. Noble words. And true. But sometimes not quite so easy to follow.

Meanwhile life went on. The seven dwarfs went off to work every day, secure in the knowledge that at the end of the day they could come home to a comfortable house and a hot meal. Their little woman, Snow-White, would provide for their every need. They were content.

But "*during the day the girl was alone.*"

THE TEXT

Now the queen, believing that she had eaten Snow-White's lungs and liver, could only think that she was again the first and the most beautiful woman of all. She stepped before her mirror and said: "Mirror, mirror, on the wall, who in this land is fairest of all?"

It answered: "You, my queen, are fair; it is true. But Snow-White, beyond the mountains with the seven dwarfs, is still a thousand times fairer than you."

This startled the queen, for she knew that the mirror did not lie, and she realized that the huntsman had deceived her, and that Snow-White was still alive. Then she thought, and thought again, how she could kill Snow-White, for as long as she was not the most beautiful woman in the entire land her envy would give her no rest.

Chapter 8: Ego and Envy

Now the queen, believing that she had
eaten Snow-White's lungs and liver,
could only think that she was again the first
and the most beautiful woman of all.
She stepped before her mirror and said:
"Mirror, mirror, on the wall, who in this
land is fairest of all?"
It answered: "You, my queen, are fair; it is
true. But Snow-White, beyond the
mountains with the seven dwarfs, is still a
thousand times fairer than you."
This startled the queen, for she knew that
the mirror did not lie,
and she realized that the huntsman had
deceived her,
and that Snow-White was still alive.

E go can be insatiable. It feeds way past the point of nourishment. It can, and often does, devour its host. Queen Ego, having thought she dealt once and for all with the troubling matter of Primal Soul, stood again before her mirror, expecting to admire herself.

It's time to pause for a moment and review where we have been and where we are going. Remember that the story of *Little Snow-White* is a metaphor. In it we find symbols that resonate with our culture's method of operation.

But it is also extremely personal. It describes how many people, maybe even most people, approach life today. We all need to constantly ask ourselves probing questions: "How much does Ego drive me? Who is really in control of my life? What motivates my actions?" Anything short of that will give Ego a chance to take us over without our realizing it.

Remember that Ego thinks she is in control. She thinks she has given birth to Primal Soul. She also thinks she has consumed its energy.

But she is wrong. Soul is eternal. Ego is mortal. And she is terrified to be reminded of who is actually in charge. Ego dwells within the confines of the Great Illusion—the belief that what we see and experience is the "real" Reality.

But the "I," Ego, is merely a passing manifestation of the material time/space continuum.

How many times have we Ego-centered mortals said things such as this?

- "I have a heart."

- "I have a mind."

- "I have a soul."

Who is the "I" who thinks it "has" all this stuff? Plain and simple, it is Ego. Ego thinks it is in possession of these things. They are all attributes it "has." But what happens to soul, for instance, when we die?

Ego somehow thinks it will accompany soul into the afterlife. "If I die before I wake, I pray the Lord 'my' soul to take."

What kind of nonsense is this? The very idea of Ego petitioning divinity—thinking it can benevolently allow Spirit, God, The Lord, or whatever we choose to call the Source, to take "it's" soul to heaven while Ego tags along, is preposterous. Ego never "possessed" soul in the first place. If Ego's soul continues on after death, obviously soul is the one who possesses ego, not the other way around. Ego doesn't "have" a soul. Soul has a temporary body which, while it is still alive, identifies with itself as Ego.

Similarly, Ego identifies with itself as body. We pay far more money and spend far more time gratifying body and ego then we do soul. Every morning we get out of bed and groom our bodies to satisfy our egos. We care how we look. It matters to us how we appear in the mirror of our culture. We go to doctors when our bodies need healing. As a culture, we pour many billions of dollars into health care. As individuals, we put our best foot forward on social media so as to constantly appear successful, entertaining, and fun. We spend lots of money dressing up our bodies. But how much time and treasure do we spend on the nourishment of our human soul?

"How do I go about nourishing my soul?" you ask. "I don't know where to start!"

That just proves the point. There are many books and magazines dedicated to teaching us how to look good. Products galore line the shelves of supermarkets and pharmacies everywhere. But you have to really look hard to find soul-nurturing advice.

These days many specialists in the field of science employ a technique called reductionism. They seek to understand something by reducing it down to its component parts. Even doctors use this method to work with the human body. They break the body down into component organs. Each organ has its own medical specialist. That's why your family doctor merely serves as a convenient stopover on the way to a more expensive specialist somewhere else.

Organs are broken down into tissue and cells. Cells are eventually reduced to physics—to atoms and even smaller particles. In the end, having peeled all the layers off the onion of life, we discover that the primary component of all humans is, basically, nothing physical at all. We reduce the human body down to pure energy.

But that doesn't reveal who you really are, does it? You can search and probe, analyze and explore, but you can't find a specific organ that appreciates beauty or is capable of abstract thought and philosophical understanding. Although it appears all of that takes place in the brain, the brain is really nothing more than electro-chemical components that transfer information. We don't appreciate and contemplate with our brains. The best we can do is say we think with our brains. We feel with our "hearts," whatever that means.

In the end, the Ego doesn't even "have" a body. The soul does. Ego is what a body feels when it views itself in the mirror of life. Remember again that Ego isn't automatically a bad thing. It is the inevitable result of differentiation, of individuality. I am separate from you. You are separate from me. That separateness is felt and expressed by the word "I."

Primal Soul is born on earth and takes on human form in order to experience life in the material world. It deliberately seeks separateness because individuality can be experienced in no other environment. There is no individuality in the Unity of the Source. The world is a necessary, and important, even essential, training ground. But when Ego tries to dominate, when it forgets its proper place in the great scheme of things, it becomes a demon that seeks to possess its host.

If we look around today, it seems to be winning. Ego is mortal and material. Therefore, it seeks to nourish its material environment. It seeks to augment its hold. And it is doing very well in that task. It has created ever more ego-centered hosts, who have then manipulated the natural world in which they evolved.

Ego needs continuous growth. It has spent most of human history trying to separate its hosts from the natural environment that is its essential mother. Most people alive today, despite being part of a species that evolved within the embrace of nature for thousands and thousands of years, are not at one with their natural habitat. They're not even comfortable in it. Instead of Mother Nature being treated as the source of abundant life, she is raped and pillaged, ravaged for her resources.

Walled off within a wood, brick, and plaster fortress, Queen Ego gazes out the window and views the source of her salvation from afar, while Snow-White has now returned to the ground of her being, the natural world from whence she sprang. She is living *"beyond the mountains with the seven dwarfs."* Ego, thinking she has ultimately destroyed Primal Soul and fed on her energies in order to sustain and promote her own selfish agenda, realizes with horror that her arch enemy, Primal Soul, lives on. And she is afraid.

Then she thought, and thought again, how

she could kill Snow-White,

for as long as long as she was not the most

beautiful woman in the entire land her envy

would give her no rest.

Ego and envy are two sides of the same coin. Ego is nourished by envy. Envy drives Ego. Ego stares into her mirror, seeing only the illusion of what she thinks she is or must be. But envy pushes her to that mirror in the first place, convincing her that she needs reassurance every day to gratify her insatiable appetite.

There is no greater proof of the constant need for ego-boosting than that which is revealed by a quick glance at the world of today's social media frenzy. We need to know if people are thinking about us, so we look in the mirror of our Facebook presence or email account. How many views have we received today? How many emails do we have?

One of the most blatant examples of the need for ego-boosting is the daily barrage of Facebook messages in which people beg us to pass along their information so they can affirm their worth by seeing how many views they can acquire. They send us a picture of a clearly helpless animal with the caption, "I'll bet I don't get even one share," relying on pity to accumulate hits. The computers at Facebook tell us that we scored a certain number of responses last week. "Keep up the good work!" they say, or "Send out a new message. People are waiting to hear from you!"

When our email account reveals no new messages, we are convinced no one loves us anymore. We check our devices hourly in an orgy of reassurance. We try to convince ourselves that we are simply staying connected. But let's be honest. Twenty years ago, we didn't perish because we weren't constantly in touch with people. The world continued to revolve.

What changed? We became a victim of our own needs. We are now Queen Ego, staring into a mirror, asking for confirmation that we are still the fairest in the land— that people care. We are seeking self-worth through the mirror of technological culture.

Sometimes that mirror says, "You're doing well, but someone over there is doing better. They have more views. They have a bigger following. You're not measuring up."

"You, my queen, are fair; it is true. But Snow-White ... is still a thousand times fairer than you." She has a better social media presence than you do. Therefore, she must be more important. And envy whispers in our ear, "You are not the most important person in the land."

So we pull out our smart phones, take a picture of the meal we have just been served, display a map showing the location of the restaurant we are gracing with our presence, push the send button, and say to our faithful following, "Look where I am! Look what I'm doing! I'm the fairest in all the land!" And all this before we have taken the first bite.

This is nothing new. People have always wanted to "keep up with the Joneses" next door. Behemoths such as the automotive industry, for instance, have thrived by convincing us we need newer, bigger, more status-revealing cars. Marketing has always been at the forefront of sales. It's the bread and butter of the fashion industry as well. And marketing thrives on envy. All social media has done is to provoke envy, and display ego on a bigger, more visible screen. It has demonstrated to anyone with even a modicum of honest introspection that we are all Queen Ego, staring into our mirror.

With the voice of envy egging us on, Ego drags us across the boundary of a land called Narcissism. Primal Soul—Intuitive Innocence—doesn't care about such things. It has no need to keep up and keep score. It rejoices only in the experience in which it currently finds itself. This is the reason it entered the material world in the first place—to gain such experience. It has no desire to compare itself with the experience of someone or something else.

Thus it is that Queen Ego, knowing in her heart of hearts that Primal Soul was her superior, but never being honest enough admit it, sought to eliminate the competition. *"She thought, and thought again, how she could kill Snow-White."* Ego, prodded by envy, alive and well in the land of Narcissism, faced a fork in the road. Would she acquiesce, rejoice in her rightful place as #2 in her relationship with Primal Soul, and be happy, or would she plot the death of her perceived enemy?

The answer soon becomes painfully obvious. Envy would allow nothing less than total annihilation. *"Her envy would give her no rest."* She must kill that which she considered to be her adversary.

Buy more. Produce more. Spend more. Stomp on the competition. Stand alone in the end zone of life, a single finger pointing toward heaven, and declare that you are the undisputed winner. That's the way to play the game. That's the way to declare your importance. That's the way to prove your worth!

Or, at least, that's what envy convinced Ego to believe. But as we shall soon see, those rules lead only to disaster.

THE TEXT

At last, she thought of something.
Coloring her face, she disguised herself as
an old peddler woman, so that no one
would recognize her. In this disguise she
went to the house of the seven dwarfs.
Knocking on the door she called out,
"Beautiful wares for sale, for sale!"

Snow-White peered out the window
and said, "Good day, dear woman, what do
you have for sale?"

"Good wares, beautiful wares," she
answered. "Bodice laces in all colors." And
she took out one that was braided from
colorful silk. "Would you like this one?"

"I can let that honest woman in,"
thought Snow-White, then unbolted the
door and bought the pretty bodice lace.

"Child," said the old woman, "how you look! Come, let me lace you up properly."

The unsuspecting Snow-White stood before her and let her do up the new lace, but the old woman pulled so quickly and so hard that Snow-White could not breathe.

"You used to be the most beautiful one," said the old woman, and hurried away.

Not long afterward, in the evening time, the seven dwarfs came home. How terrified they were when they saw their dear Snow-White lying on the ground, not moving at all, as though she were dead. They lifted her up, and, seeing that she was too tightly laced, they cut the lace in two. Then she began to breathe a little, and little by little she came back to life.

When the dwarfs heard what had happened, they said, "The old peddler woman was no one else but the godless

queen. Take care and let no one in when
we are not with you."

Chapter 9: Duplicity

At last, she thought of something. Coloring her face, she disguised herself as an old peddler woman, so that no one would recognize her. In this disguise she went to the house of the seven dwarfs. Knocking on the door she called out,

"Beautiful wares for sale, for sale!"

Snow-White peered out the window and said,

"Good day, dear woman, what do you have for sale?"

"Good wares, beautiful wares," she answered. "Bodice laces in all colors."

And she took out one that was braided from colorful silk.

"Would you like this one?"

"I can let that honest woman in," thought Snow-White,

then unbolted the door and bought the pretty bodice lace.

S o far, we haven't had much good to say about Ego. We've painted it as the enemy to Primal Soul that it really is.

If we were communicating within a different format—say, a seminar situation—at this point I would probably stop and ask a question of the group.

"As we've progressed through the story so far, how many of you have quietly assured yourself that you've got your Ego in check pretty well—that you agree with the idea that Ego in some people can be dangerous but you are in good control of your own?"

I would be willing to hazard a guess that the majority would raise their hands. I am further willing to guess that most people reading this book, including you, have thought much the same thing.

The original author of this story probably expected the same reaction. So we are now presented with a real soul-searcher. The author tells us that Ego has probably been working on us in disguise, and we either don't, or won't, acknowledge it. "*Coloring her face, she disguised herself as an old peddler woman, so that no one would recognize her. In this disguise she went to the house of the seven dwarfs."*

Ego works best in disguise. She usually comes at us in a way we never expect. She seeks to destroy us with subterfuge. Disguising herself as a harmless old woman, one that nobody would suspect, she quietly and cleverly attacked Snow-White.

No one would submit to ego if it appeared as a raging lion. Our culture has unwritten but strict rules about that. If someone brags about their accomplishments, for instance, we are repelled, and accuse them of being ego-centric. We call them a blowhard or some such thing, and dismiss them.

But if someone quietly arranges a situation in which we think we have discovered their strengths on our own, we are so impressed that we praise them to the skies. They disguise their ego and we fall right into their trap.

I once watched this done cleverly on a TV special, in which a famous piano player, who had experienced a really big hit record years ago, was being honored. In the midst of his concert, he was about to play his hit song. Rather than saying, "Hey! This is the song that made me a star!" he looked at the audience and said, "A number of years ago I recorded a little song called (here he named the song that everyone recognized.)" Then he grinned and waited for the response he knew would come. And, of course, it did. The audience broke out into applause.

It was beautifully done. His ego got the applause it was looking for, but he didn't have to appear conceited by reminding everyone how much of a success he was. He let everyone think they had remembered how big a hit it was all by themselves. He made them feel like trivia experts and insiders who were socially attuned. He acted in a fake, but seemingly humble, manner, and thus received the coveted affirmation of his past success that he so desired.

I watched the whole episode in awe. A disguised Queen Ego had struck again.

We see it all the time:

"Hey, that's a beautiful sweater you made!"

"What? This old thing?" (If you can blush a little here it helps the effect.)

Or, "You did a great job on that project!"

"Oh, anyone could have done it." ("If they had my talent and experience!")

Ego can be diabolical in its cleverness. It is constantly disguising itself so as to appear harmless and even helpful. But all the time, it is trying to sell us its wares. And when we respond out of courtesy, "*I can let that honest woman in,*" it takes advantage of our innocent acceptance and gains entrance into our hearts.

Ego is jealous of innocence, and uses that which it seeks to destroy—the innocent goodness of the world—to devour its prey. To make things worse, ego is habitual. Once we are deceived by ego, it is very hard to recover. Some people never do. Clothed in their ego, they go to their deaths thinking they never got what they were convinced they deserved.

> *"Child," said the old woman, "how you*
> *look! Come, let me lace you up properly."*
> *The unsuspecting Snow-White stood before*
> *her and let her do up the new lace,*
> *but the old woman pulled so quickly and so*
> *hard that*

Snow-White could not breathe.
"You used to be the most beautiful one,"
said the old woman, and hurried away.

Back in 1968, I graduated from the Eastman School of Music. I was surrounded by some of the finest young musicians in the country. One of them, a few years ahead of me in school, was a very gifted flutist. She was good and she knew it. It takes a certain amount of ego to be a world class musician, and this young woman had enough to see her through, without a doubt. We could all see that she was exceptionally good, and deferred to her because she could obviously back up whatever claims she made. Upon graduation most of us went about the often-humiliating process of auditions, and were quite happy whenever a job, any job, opened up. We were quite content to pay our dues, knowing we needed a certain amount of experience playing with less than top orchestras and ensembles before we were ready for prime time.

Not this classmate. She was going to hold out for a job with an orchestra that matched her talents. But this was 1968. Women were just starting to break in at the top positions in premiere orchestras. Even as late as 1996,

Maestro Zubin Mehta was quoted in the New York Times: "I just don't think women should be in an orchestra," said Mehta, whose Los Angeles Philharmonic had a total of only 16 women members at the time. "They become men. Men treat them as equals. They even change their pants in front of them. I think it's terrible!"

My colleague from Eastman was turned down by every orchestra for which she auditioned. She insisted, I heard much later, that the reason for her rejection was not her lack of talent, but her gender. She was probably right. But her ego would not permit her to be a patient groundbreaker. Safely clothed in the garb of a persecuted woman, this talented performer eventually moved back home to live with her parents.

A year went by. Then two. Then five. Eventually she lost her edge. As far as I know, she never did make it to the big time. But I know a lot of other less talented musicians from my class who did. Not right away, of course. For many reasons, they had to wait their turn. Usually, the reasons were that they had talent but lacked experience. So they kept plugging away, taking lesser jobs that didn't quite pay the bills, teaching music lessons to neighborhood kids, gathering needed experience all the time.

It was ego that kept this young musician back, not talent. Ego, disguised as cultural bias, got in her front door and sold her a pile of wares that eventually devoured her, choking off a lot of ability that could have been appreciated and enjoyed by the whole world. Envy ate away at her. In the end, her musical talent, which she had always used in competitive rather than artistic ways, consumed her. She clothed herself with the wares of Ego, and got cinched up tight. It choked the artistic life out of her.

Thus does Ego ever seek to squeeze the life out of its host.

Not long afterward, in the evening time, the
seven dwarfs came home.
How terrified they were when they saw
their dear Snow-White lying on the ground,
not moving at all, as though she were dead.
They lifted her up, and, seeing that she was
too tightly laced, they cut the lace in two.

Then she began to breathe a little, and little
by little she came back to life.

The Keepers of the Sacred Flame saved Primal Soul from death. Cosmic serendipity came to her rescue and freed her from the restraints of Ego's embrace.

I wish my flutist friend had listened to her own Keepers of the Sacred Flame, those people who could have taken her aside and whispered in her ear, explaining to her that her ego had bound her tightly and was choking the creative talent out of her. The dwarfs, remember, are symbolic of those helpful folks who live in society and appreciate the beauty inherent in Primal Soul, even if they sometimes fall short of its ideals.

We all have people like that in our lives. Maybe it's the voice of a teacher or mentor, perhaps even a good friend. My musical colleague must have had someone who could have advised her to go slow and wait for her break to come. Her talent might have been in such demand that she could have used it to become a formidable frontline force against the practice of patriarchy in the world of music. She might have been able to pave the way for the next generation of female superstars. Instead, she wasted her opportunity and allowed ego to choke out her spark.

Not so with Snow-White. The Keepers of the Sacred Flame freed her from her restrictions and watched as life returned. Ego was defeated for the time being, but would soon return.

That's the way it is in life. The battle against oppressive ego is one that continues until our bodies draw their last breath and we retire forever from its embrace. As a matter of fact, sometimes it gets harder as we get older. The successful person who retires from the field in which their success was earned sometimes discovers that adoring underlings no longer care about their achievements.

Even worse, with technological change happening so quickly these days, sometimes a person who has worked in a particular field for their whole life can find themselves suddenly obsolete, and cast aside. Their picture may still hang in the corporate office hallway, but their talents are no longer required. That can be difficult to swallow, and ego is always ready to pounce.

For five years at the end of my career, I lived in a Florida community for people who were over 55 years old.

There were quite a few captains of industry who were my neighbors, and I enjoyed, at least until it got pretty tiring, seeing how they responded to life in the slow lane. I discovered that one of two responses were the norm.

Sometimes men who had been in charge of corporate committees and boards, who had wielded great power and were accustomed to see people jump when they told them to, channeled all that executive energy into every neighborhood committee they could join. They never ceased to tell their fellow board members "how we used to do it back up north." They were often real terrors, thorns in the sides of park administrators, who were just trying to do their jobs for the good of all the people in the community.

Other men reacted differently. Those who had once overseen great projects and million-dollar real estate deals poured all their energy into their front lawns. It seemed to me that some of them named every blade of grass. I guess this is quite common across the country. Otherwise, why would the grumpy old man who shouts, "Hey you kids! Stay off my lawn!" be such a universal Hollywood staple in movies? Sometimes it feels as if all we have left is a few blades of grass.

It's hard to retire from the excitement and challenge of an important position and just leave it all behind. Our ego is used to constant feedback from the mirror of professional life. It doesn't stop its demands just because we decide to leave the mainstream. Controlling ego is a major concern throughout life. It is always in the wings, waiting to pounce.

When the dwarfs heard what had
happened, they said,
"The old peddler woman was no one else
but the godless queen.
Take care and let no one in when we are
not with you."

The Keepers of the Sacred Flame, having rescued Primal Soul once, warned her to watch out. Their victory was only temporary. Ego would certainly return.

But notice the interesting choice of words. Ego is recognized as "*the godless queen.*" When the dwarfs first saw Snow-White, they called out, "*Oh, good heaven! Oh, good heaven!*" They recognized where Primal Soul had come from—Heaven, the abode of God. Now they contrast Primal Soul with a "godless" queen.

The author seems to be telling us that in this life we are, practically if not spiritually, separated from the Holy by an Ego that places itself before divinity. It is, in effect, "godless." If Eden, the Source, is a place of unity, the world we now inhabit is a place of separation. We are separated from each other when we acknowledge "I" and "you." We are separated from our natural environment when we seek to exploit nature rather than revere it. And we are separated from Spirit when our minds require proof, rather than faith.

The old hymn, written by a forgotten composer, captures the whole experience very well: "You have to walk this lonesome valley by yourself. Nobody else can walk it for you." The "lonesome valley" of life is for individuals to experience. But the "walk" doesn't last forever. It will end someday. And when it does, Ego will have served its sometimes-contorted purpose, while Primal Soul will return to its destiny, which was its origin as well.

THE TEXT

When the wicked queen returned home, she went to her mirror and asked: "Mirror, mirror, on the wall, who in this land is fairest of all?"

The mirror answered once again: "You, my queen, are fair; it is true. But Snow-White, beyond the mountains with the seven dwarfs, is still a thousand times fairer than you."

When she heard that, all her blood ran to her heart because she knew that Snow-White had come back to life.

"This time," she said, "I shall think of something that will destroy you."

Then with the art of witchcraft, which she understood, she made a poisoned comb. Then she disguised herself, taking the form of a different old woman. Thus, she went across the seven mountains to the seven dwarfs, knocked on the door, and called out, "Good wares for sale, for sale!"

Snow-White looked out and said, "Go on your way. I am not allowed to let anyone in."

"You surely may take a look," said the old woman, pulling out the poisoned comb and holding it up. The child liked it so much that she let herself be deceived, and she opened the door.

After they had agreed on the purchase, the old woman said, "Now let me comb your hair properly."

She had barely stuck the comb into Snow-White's hair when the poison took effect, and the girl fell down unconscious.

"You specimen of beauty," said the wicked woman, "now you are finished." And she walked away.

Fortunately, it was almost evening, and the seven dwarfs came home. When they saw Snow-White lying on the ground as if she were dead, they immediately suspected the queen. They examined her and found the poisoned comb. They had scarcely pulled it out when Snow-White came to herself again and told them what had happened. Once again, they warned her to be on guard and not to open the door for anyone.

Chapter 10: A Different Strategy

When the wicked queen returned home, she
went to her mirror and asked: "Mirror,
mirror, on the wall, who in this land is
fairest of all?"
The mirror answered once again: "You, my
queen, are fair; it is true.
But Snow-White, beyond the
mountains with the seven dwarfs,
is still a thousand times fairer than you."
When she heard that, all her blood ran to
her heart because she knew that
Snow-White had come back to life.
"This time," she said, "I shall think of
something that will destroy you."

E go is relentless. It doesn't know the meaning of the word, "enough." All it understands is "more." And its chief admirer is nothing less than itself.

Earlier, we made reference to the word narcissism. In Greek mythology, Narcissus was a young man who once caught a glimpse of himself reflected in a still pool of water. He became entranced with his own image and couldn't tear himself away from gazing at his visage. Eventually he wasted away while staring at the image of himself in the water. After his death he made his way to the river Styx for the traditional boat ride to Hades. The boatman noticed however, that even here the shade of Narcissus kept leaning over the side of the boat, staring into the waters over which they passed, searching for his reflection. Ever since then, people who can't get enough of themselves have been called Narcissists.

This is a good description of Queen Ego. "*When the wicked queen returned home, she went to her mirror and asked: "Mirror, mirror, on the wall, who in this land is fairest of all?"* Thinking she had disposed of Little Snow-White, the very first thing she did when she got home was to look in her mirror to view her reflection.

In light of what we had to say earlier about Facebook and Emails being a narcissistic, ego-boosting endeavor, how many of us need to pause and ask ourselves what we do the first thing in the morning when we get out of bed or the last thing we do before retiring. Do we haul out our smart phones or computers and gaze into the mirror of its reflective surface to see ourselves through the lens of our social culture? No matter how much we tell ourselves that we are just staying in touch, do we secretly hope that someone has been thinking about us? Are we seeking assurance that we matter, by looking for approval in the mirror of culture? If so, maybe we need to ask how deeply Queen Ego has infiltrated our very being. According to Greek mythology, narcissism will kill you in the end.

Having discovered that her plans had once again failed, Ego would not rest. Primal Soul lived on. "*When she heard that, all her blood ran to her heart because she knew that Snow-White had come back to life. 'This time,' she said, 'I shall think of something that will destroy you'.*"

Ego has now been totally consumed by one thing, and one thing only. She must live, and Primal Soul must die.

Then with the art of witchcraft, which she understood, she made a poisoned comb. Then she disguised herself, taking the form of a different old woman. Thus, she went across the seven mountains to the seven

dwarfs, knocked on the door, and called
out, "Good wares for sale, for sale!"
Snow-White looked out and said,
"Go on your way. I am not allowed to let
anyone in."
"You surely may take a look," said the old
woman,
pulling out the poisoned comb and holding
it up.
The child liked it so much that she let
herself be deceived,
and she opened the door.

It's interesting to note that the weapon Ego chose to attack Primal Soul was a familiar one. Ego is very well acquainted with pride and vanity. That was made obvious every time she stood before her mirror. And it was pride and vanity that Queen Ego used to poison Primal Soul. Snow-White was proud of her beautiful hair. She was immediately attracted to the comb. And that attraction nearly caused her death.

We need to be really careful here. There is nothing wrong with combing your hair. There is nothing inherently dangerous about the practice itself. It's even an important activity. But the point of the story is that this wasn't a simple comb. It had been poisoned by Ego.

What this means is that although we earlier seemed to condemn activities involving, for instance, social media, the media is not, in and of itself, inherently a bad thing. It becomes dangerous only when we allow Ego to poison it and turn it into a weapon. In other words, one person's healthy social connections can become another person's poisoned downfall. The danger lies not in the activity. The danger lies in how we use that activity.

Ego constantly attacks us at the point of our pride and vanity. And it always comes in disguise. It is dangerous because sometimes we do not recognize its form until it is too late.

It is a good thing to cultivate a talent, for instance. It's good to become really expert at something, even to the point of being set apart from others and recognized for a unique and helpful ability. Used correctly, such an ability can be used to help our communities.

But if we become overly proud, and even conceited, thinking our ability is more important than someone else's, we become vulnerable to attack. Once we fall victim to ego's disguised wiles, it becomes habitual. And, as everyone knows who has fallen under a bad habit's spell, sometimes we are the last to recognize it in ourselves.

Ego always attacks at the point of our pride. It seems impossible that such a transparent ruse could not be seen, interpreted, and foresworn. But when ego is in control, we do the dumbest things. It's almost like magic, or "*the art of witchcraft, which she understood.*" Lives have been destroyed because people followed ego's siren call rather than common sense. It's as if ego casts a spell over us, and we follow her off a cliff.

In the case of Snow-White, Queen Ego was able to appeal to her vanity. Snow-White was proud of her hair. All it took was a glimpse of a comb and she was hooked. "*The child liked it so much that she let herself be deceived, and she opened the door.*"

Notice the words, "*she let herself be deceived.*" It wasn't entirely the queen's doing. It never is entirely ego's fault. We play our part as well. Ego is always around, offering her wares. And sometimes we are too quick to buy them. Snow-White did not realize that pride is poisonous.

When the ancients said that "pride goeth before a fall," they knew what they were talking about. I was taught a lesson in humility many years ago during an episode in my life I call the Great Booth Bay Revival. Queen Ego got me really good in that one.

Back in the days when I was a fundamentalist Christian, I used to lead what Southerners call revivals. A church would ask me to come for a series of meetings, sometimes a few days, sometimes a week, lead services every night, meet with small groups during the day, sing a little, preach a lot, and try to lead people into a deeper spiritual life.

By the time of the Great Booth Bay Revival, I had recorded and sold a few thousand copies of two gospel music albums and led perhaps two or three hundred revivals. Moody Bible Institute, a bastion of Midwestern fundamentalism, had even flown a man out from Chicago to talk to me about applying for a music position in their organization. When he saw my beard, he probably pegged me for a radical, so that didn't pan out. But I was still pretty confident. So when I got a call from an enthusiastic pastor in Booth Bay to come and revitalize the spiritual condition of the Maine seacoast, I was ready.

The plan was to go down to Maine (Real New Englanders go "down" to Maine, not up. It refers back to the seafaring days when Maine was downwind from Boston.), do a concert on Wednesday, then lead church services for the next four nights, culminating on Sunday evening, with a real revival camp meeting, featuring foot-stamping music and an altar call in the spirit of Billy Graham.

About two months before the event, the pastor called to ask if I could send some record albums to the local country music radio station. They had promised air time each day during their "Song of Inspiration" segment.

I was only too happy to oblige.

A few weeks later, I was asked to supply some posters. The church was going to blanket the town in a technique they called saturation evangelism.

You want posters? I got 'em!

A week before the event, the local newspaper asked for some 8 X 10 glossies.

Sure! Fire off the photos.

The morning of the first meeting, I loaded up my motor home with sound equipment, instruments, records and tapes, and sallied forth to change the course of religious life in America.

By the time I hit Booth Bay I was seeing my face on posters plastered to every tree and telephone pole in the area. With exquisite timing, as I pulled into the church parking lot, I found the local station on the AM dial just as they were playing the last verse of me singing "In the Garden."

The pastor met me and helped me set up my equipment and do a sound check. Then it was off to dinner at his house. After a light supper we shared some fervent prayer in his office and then headed into the sanctuary. I walked in the back door promptly at 7:30 to meet the congregation that was to occupy my activities for the next four days.

The total crowd consisted of the pastor and his family, my wife and me, the organist, five members of the Ladies Benevolent Society, who were meeting that night anyway and decided to stay for the service, and a custodian who spent most of the hour looking at his watch!

The first hymn of the evening, sung falteringly, if not ironically, by the assembled multitude, was, "Faith is the Victory that Overcomes the World."

Now, to be fair, the congregations did get bigger. I assume the church members were somewhat embarrassed and spread the word. By Sunday the church was pretty much filled. They were wonderful people and I really enjoyed my stay with them. But my first thought as I entered the sanctuary that Wednesday night was, "Pride goeth before a fall!" I had groomed my spiritual hair with Ego's poisoned comb, and it knocked me for a loop.

Ego works hard, even when we are very young, to infiltrate our lives and entangle us in its poisonous embrace. Watch a young boy shooting a basketball all by himself, for instance. Listen to what he is saying. He's not just trying to get the ball through the basket. He's playing to an imaginary audience.

"He shoots! He scores! He wins the game in the last second!"

The boy sees himself as a hero and a champion. There's nothing wrong with that. After all, he's just a kid trying to visualize the athlete he'd like to become.

The problem comes when he carries his imaginary audience with him into adulthood and lives his life as though people are really cheering his every move. When he acts out of that mindset, ego has permeated his defenses. He thinks the world revolves around him. When he learns the truth, discovering that no one really cares and that the world will continue in orbit whether or not he even exists, it can be devastating. Ego will have poisoned him.

After they had agreed on the purchase, the
old woman said,
"Now let me comb your hair properly."
She had barely stuck the comb into Snow-
White's hair when the poison took effect,
and the girl fell down unconscious.
"You specimen of beauty," said the wicked
woman, "now you are finished."
And she walked away.

Mortal Ego recognizes the eternal beauty in Primal Soul. But rather than rejoice in the fact that it is privileged to share a life, even though it may seem to be a brief one, with eternal, intuitive innocence, rather than being a proud parent who is able to take justly deserved pride in the growth experiences of its offspring, it brooks no challengers. Anything that threatens ego must die. *"She had barely stuck the comb into Snow-White's hair when the poison took effect, and the girl fell down unconscious. 'You specimen of beauty,' said the wicked woman, 'now you are finished'."*

There are many people in today's world, especially people of privilege, who have never had to experience life on the edge of despair, poverty, ill health, persecution, or discrimination, who have fallen victim to ego's poison, and carry that poison with them to their graves. A real ego-maniac is already dead, but doesn't realize it. You see it most vividly in those who live their lives habitually in the public eye. Sometimes they are entertainers or politicians. Sometimes they are captains of industry who mistake a lucky break for their own creative genius.

How do we spot it in ourselves? How do we keep from succumbing to ego's relentless attempts to poison our lives?

Once again, we need to trust the Keepers of the Sacred Flame.

Fortunately, it was almost evening, and the
seven dwarfs came home.
When they saw Snow-White lying on the
ground as if she were dead,
they immediately suspected the queen.
They examined her and found the poisoned
comb.
They had scarcely pulled it out when Snow-
White came to herself again
and told them what had happened.
Once again, they warned her to be on
guard and not to open the door for anyone.

The Keepers of the Sacred Flame are, in one important way, similar to Queen Ego. They both recognize the beauty inherent in Primal Soul. The difference is that the dwarfs, even though they fall short, at least try to walk the path of intuitive innocence. Ego seeks to destroy. The dwarfs try to protect.

We need to pay close attention to those around us in order to differentiate between the two. Our family, close friends, and advisors—our Keepers of the Sacred Flame—

may not be perfect examples of intuitive innocence themselves, but if we hear overtones in their patterns of speech that warn us of encroaching ego, we need to be alert.

A few chapters ago I shared a piece called *Timothy's Story: A Fantasy for Troubled Times.* Let me highlight a small portion here, to serve as an illustration:

More and more, Tim was asked to speak at national corporate meetings in many different industries. Over and over again he told his story, preaching the gospel he called the spiritual principles of corporate success. In the process he had a tremendous effect on the market place. Companies slowly came to the conclusion that they had to treat their employees with dignity, respect, and trust if they wanted to attract the best and brightest. The *Today Show*, capitalizing on his religion degree, introduced him as the "Motivational Maharishi."

Alicia didn't let it go to his head,

though. She started calling him "Yogi." "Hey Yogi, get your face out of your press clippings and get over here. I need help with this!" Much to Tim's chagrin, the name stuck. But secretly, he kind of liked it.

When Tim started to get publicity, it could very well have poisoned his attitude. Ego might have destroyed him. In this case, Alicia served as his Keeper of the Sacred Flame. Her gentle sarcasm saved him from ego's embrace. And "secretly, he kind of liked it."

We all need advisors, mentors, teachers, or friends who keep us grounded. The secret is to listen to them rather than resent them. Sometimes, that's not an easy task.

In Snow-White's case, her dwarf friends warned her once again. The Keepers of the Sacred Flame told her to beware, but she refused to listen, and once again fell under Ego's spell.

THE TEXT

Back at home the queen stepped before her mirror and said: "Mirror, mirror, on the wall, who in this land is fairest of all?"

The mirror answered: "You, my queen, are fair; it is true. But Snow-White, beyond the mountains with the seven dwarfs, is still a thousand times fairer than you."

When the queen heard the mirror saying this, she shook and trembled with anger, "Snow-White shall die," she shouted, "if it costs me my life!"

Then she went into her most secret room—no one else was allowed inside—and she made a poisoned apple. From the outside it was beautiful, white with red cheeks, and anyone who saw it would want it. But anyone who might eat a little piece of it would die.

Then, coloring her face, she disguised herself as a peasant woman, and thus went across the seven mountains to the seven dwarfs. She knocked on the door.

Snow-White stuck her head out the window and said, "I am not allowed to let anyone in. The dwarfs have forbidden me to do so."

"That is all right with me," answered the peasant woman. "I'll easily get rid of my apples. Here, I'll give you one of them."

"No," said Snow-White, "I cannot accept anything."

"Are you afraid of poison?" asked the old woman. "Look, I'll cut the apple in two. You eat the red half, and I shall eat the white half."

Now, the apple had been so artfully made that only the red half was poisoned.

Chapter 11: The Great Illusion

Back at home the queen stepped before her
mirror and said:
"Mirror, mirror, on the wall, who in this
land is fairest of all?"
The mirror answered: "You, my queen, are
fair; it is true.
But Snow-White, beyond the mountains
with the seven dwarfs,
is still a thousand times fairer than you."
When the queen heard the mirror saying
this, she shook and trembled with anger,
"Snow-White shall die," she shouted, "if it
costs me my life!"

As the story continues, we witness the deteriorating facade of a desperate ego that fears it is fighting a losing battle. When ego feeds on itself in an effort to survive, it turns pathological.

Consider Ego's growing paranoia in her responses so far to the messages of the mirror:

- The first time, Ego got the response it was searching for, and "*she was satisfied, for she knew that the mirror spoke the truth.*"

- The second time, when told there was a rival to her throne, "*The queen took fright and turned yellow and green with envy.*" This marked the beginning of a long process. Envy was awakened and began to whisper in her ear.

- The third time, Ego turned feelings into obsessive thoughts. "*She thought, and thought again, how she could kill Snow-White, for as long as she was not the most beautiful woman in the entire land, her envy would give her no rest.*" She entered the realm of sleepless nights, of tossing and turning, of plotting and scheming.

- The fourth time, "*When she heard that, all her blood ran to her heart because she knew that Snow-White had come back to life. 'This time,' she said, 'I shall think of something that will destroy you'.*" Her thoughts became so poisonous that she sought revenge, as if the very idea of not being Number 1 was a personal affront and mortal insult.

- Now came the final phase. Full-fledged pathology reared its ugly head. She was consumed by gnawing envy. She vowed to right what she saw as a wrong, or die in the process. *"'Snow-White shall die,' she shouted, 'if it costs me my life!'"*

Anyone who has ever become obsessed with something or someone who was seen as a bully, a rival, or an impediment to a career or desire, knows how dangerous a moment like this can be. We even have a name for it. We call it "going postal."

On August 20, 1986, a US Postal Service Employee named Patrick Sherrill walked into his home office, shot and killed 14 co-workers, wounded six more, and then committed suicide. On October 10, 1991, Joseph Harris, a former postal worker, killed two employees at the Ridgewood, New Jersey post office. One month later, Thomas McIlvaine, after being fired from his postal service job, killed four people and then himself at a post office in Dearborn, Michigan.

It wasn't long before the press, recognizing a trend, invented a slang expression for anyone who became uncontrollable, often to the point of murder and death, in a workplace environment. The phrase, "going postal," entered the modern lexicon. It describes a situation in which someone who perceives a slight or insult, often for deserving reasons, proceeds to escalate the problem until they decide the only thing to do is to threaten, harm, or even kill, those who they see as the cause of their so-called persecution.

This is nothing new. Queen Ego has been acting out this scenario for a long, long time. One step leads to another. If unchecked, nothing will stop the process. "Death before (supposed) dishonor." It's a road that leads to tragedy.

Then she went into her most secret room—
no one else was allowed inside—
and she made a poisoned apple.
From the outside it was beautiful, white
with red cheeks,
and anyone who saw it would want it.
But anyone who might eat a little piece of it
would die.

Apples hold quite a unique position in mythology. They have a long, rich, tradition in terms of being used as metaphors. Ever since "Eve ate the apple" in the garden of

Eden, they have shown up everywhere wearing the guise of forbidden fruit.

Of course, the "apple" in the garden of Eden is actually an example of fake news. The Bible never says it was an apple. It was the "fruit of the tree of the knowledge of good and evil." But that just proves the prevalence of apples in mythology. Everyone assumes the biblical story involved an apple, because apples are so common in stories such as these.

The misunderstanding is so prevalent that the human larynx is, to this day, called an "Adam's apple" because of the belief that when Eve gave the forbidden fruit, thought to be an apple, to Adam, he choked on it. It stuck in his throat and remains there to this day, a constant reminder of the human propensity to disobey God.

But there may be a good reason for the prevalence of metaphorical apples down through history. Until the late 17th century, the word "apple" was quite a generic term. Almost every fruit of every tree was called an apple. Sometimes the term was even used to describe nut trees. Hence, acorns were called "oak apples." Tomatoes were referred to as "love apples. The "pomme de terre," or potato, is an "apple of the earth." There is even one Old English reference to the cucumber, calling it an "eorbaeppla," or "earth apple." Some languages refer to oranges as "golden apples," or sometimes "Chinese apples." Datura is a "thorn-apple."

Which brings us to an extremely interesting reference to apples that might have a direct bearing on our story. In his book, *Magic Mushrooms in Religion and Alchemy*, Clark Heinrich points out that the word "apple" in mythology is often used to describe the fly agaric mushroom. This is the so-called "magic mushroom" or psychedelic mushroom, often used by shamans to aid them in their quest for out of body states.

40,000 years ago, our human ancestors navigated what has recently been called the "great leap forward" into symbolic thought. This refers to a mind/spirit journey that led to the first animistic religion. This in the belief that everything in nature is "animated" by its own unique spirit. Evidence is found in the great painted caves of western Europe that shamanic practitioners underwent a spiritual transformation in that they became aware of parallel dimensions and realities. They recorded their visions on cave walls, thus producing the first examples of art known to archeologists.

What caused our ancestors to make this leap is unknown, but one good possibility is that they discovered hallucinogenic mushrooms and plants which, when combined in the right doses, could break down barriers in the mind.

Up to this point in history, evolution had blinded humans to realities that didn't expressly help them survive in their usual environment. It wouldn't have been advantageous for a shaman, for instance, to be mentally distracted by alternate realities when a lion was creeping up on him through the brush. The shaman's senses may not have perceived the need to contemplate such things as a Multiverse or parallel dimensions, but that was a good thing. It was very practical.

But the Multiverse, whether shamans could interact with it or not, was still there, and they eventually developed an existence safe enough to allow them to contemplate such things as eternity and infinity.

In other words, magic mushrooms—sometimes called "apples"—may have enabled our ancestors to bypass their five senses and interact with spiritual dimensions of reality. The field of metaphysics, the branch of science and philosophy that deals with abstract concepts such as being, knowing, reality, identity, time, and space, was discovered.

To bring this into focus, when Snow-White is presented with a poisoned apple, we are immediately reminded of mythological motifs involving alternate states of reality. She is about to experience the Great Illusion of death.

Snow-White, and Eve of the Garden of Eden story, weren't the only ones to interact with an apple. The golden apples of the Garden of Hesperides were also associated with knowledge, immortality, temptation, and the "fall" of humans from grace.

In Greek mythology, the Garden of Hesperides grew golden apples which were a gift from Gaia, the Earth Mother, to the goddess Hera and her husband, Zeus, on their wedding day. The garden was protected by the Hesperides, nymphs of the far west who were the daughters of Atlas, the Titan who supported the vault of heaven on his shoulders.

So it was that with a potent mythological symbol in hand, mortal Queen Ego was about to strike at immortal Primal Soul. At stake was nothing less than life or death.

Then, coloring her face, she disguised
herself as a peasant woman,
and thus went across the seven mountains
to the seven dwarfs.
She knocked on the door.
Snow-White stuck her head out the window
and said,
"I am not allowed to let anyone in. The
dwarfs have forbidden me to do so."
"That is all right with me," answered the
peasant woman.
"I'll easily get rid of my apples. Here, I'll
give you one of them."
"No," said Snow-White, "I cannot accept
anything."
"Are you afraid of poison?" asked the old
woman.
"Look, I'll cut the apple in two.

You eat the red half, and I shall eat the
white half."
Now, the apple had been so artfully made
that only the red half was poisoned.

Donning yet another disguise, the now pathologically disturbed Queen Ego made her diabolical move. She became the serpent of Eden, offering temptation as a free choice, while knowing the outcome was sure. She held in her hand the forbidden fruit.

Snow-White wavers. "*I am not allowed to let anyone in. The dwarfs have forbidden me to do so.*" But with a mixture of magic and deceit, the deed was done.

Half of the apple was safe. Half was poisoned. Significantly, Ego's deception is so subtle that it's easy to miss what's going on here.

The apple came with two faces. One was white, the other red. Remember the meanings of these colors when we first came across them. Red was the color of blood—the color of sacrifice. White was the color of purity. Red was associated with the evil queen. White with Snow-White. Her very name reveals the identification.

So eager was Queen Ego to destroy Primal Soul that she offered Snow-White the very thing that brought Ego down in the first place. The red half of the apple, Ego's color, was poisoned. The white half, the color of Primal Soul, was not. But Ego tricked Primal Soul into consuming that which is associated with the evil queen. Primal Soul's downfall happens when it is deceived into following Ego's path to destruction.

Deception is always ego's method of operation. We are never forced to fall victim to its wiles. We are always tempted. We choose to let ego have its way with us because the benefits of pleasure and recognition seem to outweigh the suffering of rejection and loneliness.

It's that simple. We know, for instance, that the rewards of receiving a good paycheck will bring material wealth, so we keep working for a company whose goals are not in line with our own ethics. We know hanging out with the wrong people is a bad thing, but we enjoy the feeling of being a part of the in-crowd. We know cheating on an exam will circumnavigate the very learning the exam is designed to test, but the results promise a short-cut to a passing grade, even if we don't deserve it. The thief steals because the reward is thought to outweigh the risk of getting caught.

And so it goes. We are constantly being offered an apple that is half good and half poisoned. And the choice goes on forever. We have to make it every day we live this life. What could be so wrong with eating an apple? Disguised Ego is eating it. Why shouldn't we? What could go wrong? It looks so good. The anticipated pleasure of its taste surpasses the advice we have been given by the Keepers of the Sacred Flame. And we succumb.

THE TEXT

Snow-White longed for the beautiful apple, and when she saw that the peasant woman was eating part of it, she could no longer resist, and she stuck her hand out and took the poisoned half. She barely had a bite in her mouth when she fell to the ground dead.

The queen looked at her with a gruesome stare, laughed loudly, and said, "White as snow, red as blood, black as ebony wood! This time the dwarfs cannot awaken you."

Chapter 12: Duality

Snow-White longed for the beautiful apple,
and when she saw that the peasant woman
was eating part of it, she could no longer
resist, and she stuck her hand out and took
the poisoned half.
She barely had a bite in her mouth when
she fell to the ground, dead.

The two-sided apple is a symbol of the world of duality in which we live. "Duality" refers to pairs of opposites. For every up there is a down, for every left, a right. Cold cannot exist except in comparison to heat—joy without the contrast of sorrow. Usually, one half of every pair of opposites is uncomfortable. The other is desirable. The natural human tendency is to identify with that which is good, comfortable, or rewarding.

Most world religions recognize this principle, and teach us to identify with the good while avoiding the bad. Monotheistic religions that teach the traditional Garden of

Eden story, for instance, insist that eating the apple was evil, an affront to God, and worthy of punishment.

But there is at least one profound spiritual tradition that leads us down a different path. It involves the teaching of Siddhartha Gautama, the Buddha, and involves following what he called The Middle Way.

In this system of thought, unless both poles of opposites are recognized and acknowledged, we cannot be content, because both poles are real, and make up the fabric of life. To remain insulated from one pole or the other is to live in denial.

What we are about to examine is a difficult concept, so let's first jump to the bottom line. We're going to ask if Primal Soul's eating of the apple, succumbing to temptation, was a necessary part of her development.

On the one hand, she was deceived. She was duped. But on the other, she had been warned, and on some level knew what she was doing was wrong, and so risked real trouble. With this in mind, consider her actions.

We all, from time to time, look back on our lives and wonder if we made the right choices. Did we marry for love or for convenience? Did we stay too long on a dead-end job? Should we have taken more risks, or should we have held back? How might our lives have been different?

Sometimes this retrospective analysis leads to guilt. Sometimes it tears us up. Some people wish they had done things differently. Others insist they wouldn't have changed a thing.

What I am going to suggest is that these questions may be meaningless. What happened, happened. The question is, how will we react now? To do this we need a crash course in rudimentary Buddhism.

The Buddha came to understand a profound psychological truth that has become part of every culture on Earth. It is so common that we forget he was the first to put it into words—to frame it in a way that easily transcends culture and language. He condensed his insight into what he called Four Noble Truths:

I. All Life Is Suffering

The Buddha did not consider life to be a miserable experience. Rather, he came to understand that even in the very best of times, the most joyous moment is spoiled by the thought that it cannot last. That's why we buy insurance. Every life will come to an end. At the moment of birth, we begin our journey toward death. That cannot be escaped. It is the central truth of existence.

Fear of death is normal. It is a healthy emotion if it causes us to move back from the edge of a cliff. But whatever our reaction, that which appears to us as an ending is real. Thus, all life is darkened at least somewhat by the knowledge that it will not last. This is the central fear of Queen Ego. She knows her end in inevitable.

Acceptance of the reality of life's end is not necessarily tragic, however. Death is a part of life. Perhaps its existence even spices up the good times a bit. So what causes suffering?

II. Suffering Is Caused by Desire

We want what we cannot have. We desire something because we believe it will bring happiness or release from sorrow. We attempt to hold on to joyous moments, trying to make them last forever. We gather things around us to protect ourselves from suffering, so life becomes a matter of accumulating and desiring more of those things—a bigger house, a more suitable mate, better clothes, a more comfortable car, a higher-paying job that will provide more money to buy more things. "Stuff" equals happiness.

But anyone who visits a modern storage facility soon understands the futility of such thinking. We buy so much "stuff" we have to pay money to keep it someplace. Where is the happiness? But still we desire more. This is the central mind-set of ego.

III. There Can Be an End to Desire

The Buddha came to realize that "desire" was the weak point in ego's armor. Suffering is like fire. It needs fuel. Remove the fuel and the fire goes out. Desire is the fuel that feeds suffering. If a person can stop desiring, he or she can stop suffering. It's as simple, and as difficult, as that.

Many Buddhists teach that people consist of five *Skandhas* (the word means "bundle.") Rather than consisting of a "soul" stuck in a body, people are formed of various layers, blending together to produce a whole. The *Skandhas* are:

227

1. Form (outward appearance)

2. Feelings (inward emotions)

3. Perceptions (how we visualize what we feel)

4. Impulses (Karmic dispositions—the forces that propel life forward toward a goal)

5. Background Consciousness (that from which we spring and to which we return)

To see how these things work together, consider, as an example, an inner conversation before buying a new car:

• *That's a nice car.* (The *form* of the car pleases us.)

• *I want that car!* (We experience an *inward emotion* of desire.)

• *I can just see myself driving down the street. Imagine the stares of approval I'd get.* (We *visualize* what we will feel.)

- *I deserve that car. It was meant for me!* (We believe *Karma*, or fate, brought us to this place and time.)

- *I was born to have a car like that!* (We come to believe our purchase is somehow *eternally predestined*.)

Form stimulates *feelings*, which induce *perceptions*, provoking *impulses*, influencing *consciousness*.

The problem is that we get stuck on the word "I." "I" want, "I" feel, "I" visualize. But who is this "I"? "I" is obviously the villain of the piece, because it is this "I" who is setting in progress the chain of desires that lead to suffering. And who is "I?" None other than our old friend, Queen Ego.

How, then, does a person stop desiring? How can we free ourselves from unrealistic expectations?

The path is difficult and fraught with irony. Zen Buddhists, for instance, sometimes teach that the only way to attain enlightenment is by not desiring it. In other words, we have to desire not to desire.

On that typically Zen note, we can proceed. Buddha's fourth noble truth offers us a guide to resisting Ego's half-poisoned apple.

IV. The Eightfold Path

There are signposts along the path of spiritual enrichment. They give directions. The Buddha traveled the path and sought to show it to others. He left us a road map. In this, he was the ultimate Keeper of the Sacred Flame.

Here are the basics—Buddhism's eight-step plan to handle the challenges of resisting temptation, or at least recognizing it when someone hands us a poisoned apple. They can be read and memorized in a few minutes. Applying them takes a lifetime.

1. Right Understanding

Right Understanding means seeing through egotistical illusions, such as the idea that wealth automatically brings happiness, or that getting older won't involve change. It has to do with seeing things as they really are, rather than as what they appear to be. It involves seeing through the Great Illusion in which we live.

2. Right Thoughts or Motives

The Buddha realized that it is not enough to do the right thing. You have to do the right thing for the right reason. Good work done for the sake of the work itself is noble. Good work done for the sake of reward or applause is nothing but self-serving ambition.

3. Right Speech

Hurtful talk hurts, even if we are the only ones to hear it. Negative words are symbols of negative thoughts. Whenever we speak negative words, our egos are thinking negative thoughts.

4. Right Action

Doing the right thing for the right reason in called integrity. When human beings *mess* up, they usually *cover* up. The recent history of politics in America has laid bare the fact that the public will forgive mistakes. What they won't forgive is lying. The real sin, at least in American politics, is not committing the act. It's covering it up.

5. Right Livelihood

A person traveling this path who abhors war cannot work for a company that manufactures weapons. A wealthy person who encourages tightening up the borders of the United States against illegal entry cannot hire illegal immigrants just because they work at substandard rates of pay. A pro-life nurse cannot work for a doctor who performs abortions. A musician who is an atheist should not be the musical director of a religious institution. A teacher who dislikes children but fears losing the security of tenure should resign.

The Buddha reminds us that what we do for a living has to be compatible with our belief system or we are living in an ego-based illusion.

6. Right Effort

It is tempting to read the Buddha's remarks, heed his advice, and then expect to make a few changes and live happily ever after. That's what our egos suggest. That will never happen. Growth is a process, not an event. It involves a lifetime of effort, not a few minutes, days, or even years.

7. Right Mindfulness

The past is memory. The future is hope. Both are subject to illusory perceptions. Our egos may have reframed the past and remember events differently from how they really happened. The future is unknowable. All we really have is this moment, right now. But many of us are so busy living in an ego-influenced past or future that we don't grasp the only thing that is real—the present moment. Right Mindfulness occurs when we live in the precise moment called *now*, and are fully aware of all that moment contains.

8. Right Meditation

The Buddha believed that it is possible for human beings to experience a final attainment of the state he called *anatman*, "no self." There we understand that we are one with everything and connected to it all, without being aware that we are aware. We simply "are."

With all this as a background, let's reconsider the situation in which Snow-White found herself. Queen Ego was not holding a knife to her throat and forcing her to eat a poisoned apple. Instead, Ego employed deception.

Snow-White faced a choice. She had been warned. She had been deceived twice before. But when given a choice, she still chose gratification over wisdom. She lived, as do we all, in a world of duality. When offered two alternatives she felt obligated to choose one, so she made the choice that felt most desirable.

In Christian theology this kind of thinking was codified by a fourth-century scholar named Augustine of Hippo. His description of the duality of good and evil laid the groundwork for virtually every Christian thinker since—including, although they are probably not aware of it, most people who simply sit in a church pew on Sunday morning, or did in their youth. He eventually became a favored theologian of sixteenth-century Protestant Reformers, and today is considered the most influential western theologian of both the Protestant and Catholic traditions.

Augustine believed that the good/evil argument lay at the very center of Christianity. If God is both good and all-powerful, how can we explain the existence of evil? How could a good God have allowed evil into the universe? Either God couldn't prevent it, in which case God was not all-powerful, or God didn't prevent it, in which case God was not good.

Augustine's solution, after studying a lot of Greek thought, dating back to the time of Socrates and Plato, was that good and evil were abstract, but very real, entities. If the Bible were to be interpreted historically, he found no difficulty in saying that human beings, ever since the original sin of Adam and Eve, brought themselves down into a sinful state by their own will.

What this meant, at least to Augustine, was that human beings are not capable of completely resisting evil. Only God can reach down through the barrier of sin, and predestine some to salvation in spite of their wickedness. Nevertheless, Augustine believed that humans must confront evil, must battle against it. This is the rationale behind the image of a devil on one shoulder and an angel on the other.

At first Augustine was confused about the fact that he rather liked the good life which seemed to be anathema to his Christian community. His used to pray, "God, give me chastity and continence, but not too soon!"

After years of intellectual and emotional struggle, Augustine persevered to finally emerge as one of the leading intellectual Christian philosophers and theologians of all times. His closely reasoned arguments against what are now called heresies, his spiritual autobiography, *Confessions*, and his monumental book, *City of God,* are still required readings at most seminaries.

The Buddha began from a similar position but then went off in a different direction. Just like Augustine, he did not deny the reality of evil, and certainly never recommended evil action. But he pointed out that since good cannot exist except as evil's opposite, there is no straight, true dividing line between the two. Human beings are not evil, but they do face an unsolvable dilemma. What is good for one person may cause evil for another. Where Augustine saw a black and white dividing line, the Buddha saw a grey tension at the very center of all life.

By embracing the reality of evil, the Buddha never suggested that people should ever commit evil acts or harm someone else. Far from it! He taught that because life consists of both good and evil, one cannot truthfully accept one and deny the other. Both exist. One person gets cancer and dies. Another survives. One person chooses to commit an evil act, another chooses not to.

That leads us to the key of this whole philosophical exercise. If Snow-White had internalized the teachings of the Buddha, she would have realized that there was a third alternative available to her. It was not a matter of good apple vs. bad apple. The third alternative was *no* apple.

Snow-White saw a presumably harmless woman, partaking of a pleasure she wanted for herself. *"When she saw that the peasant woman was eating part of it, she could no longer resist, and she stuck her hand out and took the poisoned half."*

If she had wanted to avoid a potentially bad experience, all she needed to do was keep her hands to herself and derive her own pleasure by appreciating that of another.

Instead, she ate the apple and sealed her fate.

The queen looked at her with a gruesome
stare, laughed loudly, and said,
"White as snow, red as blood, black as
ebony wood!
This time the dwarfs cannot awaken you."

Ego gloats through gruesome laughter. From the beginning, the Queen had wanted such a child. "*If only I had a child as white as snow, as red as blood, and as black as the wood in this frame*" she had said. Now her wish was fulfilled. But the child, rather than being a joy and pleasurable companion in life, had instead prompted only envy and hatred. That which the queen most wanted had become that which she most despised.

That is such an important statement that I'm going to repeat it:

That which the queen most wanted had become that which she most despised.

Such is often the case. We want something because we think it will bring us happiness. Instead, it brings only a desire for more. "If only I had ... " might be the saddest phrase ever spoken. Remember that ego doesn't know the meaning of "enough." It is never satiated, until it destroys even that which it thinks it desires.

Ultimately, though, Snow-White determined her own fate, as do we all. Sometimes even our life guides, the

Keepers of the Sacred Flames, are not enough to save us from ourselves. *"This time the dwarfs cannot awaken you!"*

A life of duality seems to constantly offer us only two choices, telling us we must desire one or the other. But the third possibility is often the wisest one. Sometimes it's best to keep our hands to ourselves, be glad to see others enjoying the fruit of our own desires, rejoice in their experience, and not choose at all.

THE TEXT

Back at home the queen asked her mirror: "Mirror, mirror, on the wall, who in this land is fairest of all?"

It finally answered: "You, my queen, are fairest of all."

Then her envious heart was at rest, as well as an envious heart can be at rest.

Chapter 13: The False Contentment of Our Age

Back at home the queen asked her mirror:
"Mirror, mirror, on the wall, who in this land is fairest of all?"
It finally answered: "You, my queen, are fairest of all."
Then her envious heart was at rest, as well as an envious heart can be at rest.

From every corner of today's world echoes a deceptive clarion call that holds us all in its seductive thrall. It announces that contentment lies just on the other side of the words, "If only."

"If only" I had a little more money ...

"If only" I had a better job ...

"If only" it wasn't for (fill in the blank) ...

"Then I would be content."

A friend meets us on the street and asks how we're doing.

"Just fine," we answer, "under the circumstances."

What, in heavens name, does that mean? Are we fine or not? If we are, then what difference does it make what our circumstances are? And why are we *under* our circumstances? What are we doing there?

Contentment can only be found *above* our circumstances. It doesn't survive *under* them. It does not exist *outside* ourselves. It can only be found *inside*.

If you live under the Great Illusion that you could be content "if only" your circumstances changed, "if only" something was different in your life, "if only" you had something you now lack, "if only" things were different, "if only" your metaphorical Snow-White was dead, then you will never find contentment.

Nothing can "bring" you contentment. At least not lasting contentment. Oh, you may find it momentarily once you obtain a sought-after treasure of some kind, be it a pay raise, a new this or a new that, recognition, or some kind of social or cultural achievement. But once the novelty wears off, discontent will return. It's like a room with a great view. After the first day or two, you don't notice it anymore.

The queen had found contentment with the supposed death of Snow-White. Having reacquired her status as "*the fairest of all*," she thought she could now be happy. "*Her envious heart was at rest.*"

But the sentence continues: "*As well as an envious heart can be at rest.*"

That's the key, isn't it? Contentment can never be ours as long as we attempt to find it by adhering to the demands of an envious heart. Fulfillment, just like happiness, real love, compassion, and every other spiritually noble ideal, can flow only from a heart that is content right now, not a heart that would be content "if only." A heart that is content now, despite the circumstances that surround it, is the key to happiness.

I used to live in Michigan, a place famous for cold, icy rains that make life miserable when, in the words of folksinger Gordon Lightfoot, "the gales of November come early." Many years ago, in the midst of one of those gales, my father and I were driving home from a thwarted Boy Scout camping trip late on a Saturday night. The heater in the car was desperately trying to ward off what we were sure would soon turn into a severe case of double pneumonia. As we turned a corner, our home neighborhood just a few blocks away, we spotted our next-door neighbor's pickup truck stalled out on the side of the road. A feeble light shone underneath and two feet, presumably belonging to somebody underneath the truck, poked out into a gathering puddle. As we stopped to ask if everything was okay, we soon discovered they belonged to none other than our neighbor, a man named Charley.

My dad rolled down the window just a crack and asked if we could offer him a ride home.

"That's okay," came Charley's cheery voice. "I've almost got it."

"It's cold out there," my dad informed him, as if he was delivering some kind of news.

"Yeah, it's a brisk night," came the reply.

"Aren't you getting wet?"

"Not anymore. I already got wet an hour ago."

"What can we do?"

Charley's face rolled out from under the truck, displaying his ever-present grin.

"Nothing. I got 'er licked now."

And Charley got into his truck, turned the key in the ignition, and listened as the engine roared into life. Then, in spite of the foul weather, he proceeded to get out, walk over to us, and start a conversation.

I admit I was curious, but I was so miserable I just wanted to get home to the cup of hot chocolate I was sure my mom would have ready and waiting.

My dad asked the question I hoped he wouldn't ask, because it would require a reply longer than I wanted to hear right then.

"Isn't this a nasty night of weather to be working on your truck?"

"Well, she quit on me a few blocks short of my garage, but I knew what the problem was, so I figured I might as well fix it right away."

"But aren't you cold and wet?"

"Sure. But that's what happens when it's November in Detroit."

He sounded as though he was no more uncomfortable cold and wet than he was hot and dry.

Now, there's a guy who can be content under any circumstances. He was just happy he could find enjoyment in a job well done. The circumstances had nothing to do with anything.

Charley is no doubt long since dead and gone. I haven't seen him since the late 1950s. But more than sixty years later I find myself still in awe of him. When it rained, he expected to get wet. That's what happens when it rains. In the winter, he expected to get cold. In the summer, he expected to be hot. No matter what the circumstances, he just kept on enjoying whatever life threw in his path.

I don't think he ever made a lot of money. To my knowledge he never became famous for anything. But he is one of my unqualified heroes. Whenever I couldn't get the lawnmower started on a Saturday morning, Charley would hear me pulling the starter cord over and over, somehow hoping that this pull would produce a different result than the one before it. He'd walk over and help me out.

248

Whenever my bike tire got flat, Charley would fix it and pump it up. When I was forced to spend one interminable summer that seemed to last for about three years because I was given the job of painting the backyard fence, Charley would show up, paintbrush in hand, and ask if he might have the honor of assisting, so I could finish my quota for the day and go play baseball with the kids. I always allowed him the privilege.

My memory is probably somewhat unreliable. I doubt he was the complete saint I remember him to be. But of all my childhood mentors, he's the one I most remember.

What does all this have to do with a queen standing in front of a mirror for her daily ego massage?

Just this. Queen Ego could only find happiness when she achieved her goal of destroying the one person she considered to be her rival. She could only be at rest "*as well as an envious heart can be at rest.*" She could not be content until she had achieved the circumstances she thought would bring her contentment.

As we shall soon see, that kind of contentment will not last.

But that's exactly what our culture teaches us from birth to death. If you haven't yet learned how to be content in any circumstances, if you are living your life *under* your circumstances rather than *above* them, if you are still waiting until your ship comes in before allowing yourself to be happy, please don't beat yourself up. You are part of a huge club. I'm a member myself. Almost all of us belong.

Ego runs amuck in our society, fed by marketing campaigns, economists, politicians, media, peer groups, friends, family, and a host of other outlets. They all speak with one voice. "You cannot be content until you have (whatever)." Fill in your own blank. We have all been deceived. We have been taught that we cannot be fulfilled until we have achieved a goal, even if that goal consists of murdering Primal Soul. Only then will we have arrived. Only then will we find peace.

But how does it profit us if we gain the whole world and lose our soul? Any benefit is strictly temporary.

All my life I harbored the secret goal that someday I wanted to retire, live in the woods for one year, watch the leaves turn colors and the seasons come and go, and finally have some free time to enjoy, all to myself. That was my goal. One year of peace and contentment. I could relax, free from schedules and commitments, and be happy for one year before I died.

I finally got all that. One year turned into more than a decade. Am I content? Well, kinda ... I mean, not quite ... but if only I had ...

See how it works? We obtain our desire and it turns into a supposed need for more.

I have come to believe that a major reason, perhaps *the* major reason, for life in the material world, is that eternal Spirit wants to teach us that materialism in any form cannot produce happiness. The only way to learn that lesson is to live it.

Apparently, this was also the view of those who wrote the scriptures shared by Jews, Christians, and Muslims. They believed that ego even brought about the downfall of angels.

In the beginning, the Bible tells us, God created a class of supernatural beings we now call angels. The word is derived from the Greek word *angelos*, or "messenger." Their purpose, apparently, was to serve God and keep him company. According to the 14th chapter of the book of

Isaiah, the leader of these heavenly entities was an angel called Lucifer, known as the "son of the morning." Unfortunately, his ego caused him to desire an even loftier position. He wanted to be like God.

This presented God with a problem. Obviously, Lucifer was quite an important angel, similar to the queen of our story. He was smart, but he didn't know everything. He missed the whole point about the fact that ego works through temptation. As a result, he "fell" from grace. He was banished to earth where his evil could be contained to one planet in the vast cosmos. A third of the heavenly host (now called demons) followed him into perdition. They now reign on earth. Hell is their punishment, not their dwelling place. Lucifer became Satan, both the "deceiver" and the "accuser of the brethren."

This is the biblical account. The first passage begins with God talking directly to Satan:

"How you have fallen from heaven, morning star, son of the dawn! You have been cast down to the earth, you who once laid low the nations!"

(Isaiah 7:14)

This next passage begins with God talking to the "King of Tyre," usually interpreted as being a metaphor for Satan:

Thus says the Lord GOD: "You were the signet of perfection, full of wisdom and perfect in beauty. You were in Eden, the garden of God; every precious stone was your covering and worked in gold were your settings and your engravings. With an anointed cherub as guardian, I placed you; you were on the holy mountain of God; you walked among the stones of fire. You were blameless in your ways from the day that you were created, until iniquity was found in you. In the abundance of your trade, you were filled with violence, and you sinned. Your heart was proud because of your beauty; you corrupted your wisdom for the sake of your splendor. By the multitude of

253

your iniquities, in the unrighteousness of your trade, you profaned your sanctuaries. So I brought out fire from within you; it consumed you, and I turned you to ashes on the earth in the sight of all who saw you. All who know you among the peoples are appalled at you; you have come to a dreadful end and shall be no more forever."

(Ezekiel 28:11-19)

And what caused this downfall? Ego! Lucifer listened to the voice of temptation. Notice how Ego's "I" enters the picture, five times:

You said in your heart, "*I will* ascend to the heavens; *I will* raise my throne above the stars of God; *I will* sit enthroned on the mount of assembly, *I will* ascend above the tops of the clouds; *I will* make myself like the Most High."

(Isaiah 14:13-15)

From these passages we learn that in the eyes of the ancients, Queen Ego wasn't the first to stare in her mirror and hope to find contentment. And she won't be the last. She enjoys a lot of company to this day. Sometimes we all take a turn. It's an old, old story.

But true contentment can only arise from a contented heart. And a contented heart can only be found in Intuitive Innocence—Primal Soul. Sometimes it appears as if she is dead and gone. But have a little faith! Appearances can be deceiving. The story is not yet over.

THE TEXT

When the dwarfs came home that evening, they found Snow-White lying on the ground. She was not breathing at all. She was dead. They lifted her up and looked for something poisonous. They undid her laces. They combed her hair. They washed her with water and wine. But nothing helped. The dear child was dead, and she remained dead. They laid her on a bier, and all seven sat next to her and mourned for her and cried for three days. They were going to bury her, but she still looked as fresh as a living person, and still had her beautiful red cheeks.

They said, "We cannot bury her in the black earth," and they had a transparent glass coffin made, so she could be seen from all sides. They laid her inside, and with golden letters wrote on it her name, and that she was a princess. Then they put the coffin outside on a mountain, and one of them always stayed with it and watched over her. The animals too came and mourned for Snow-white, first an owl, then a raven, and finally a dove.

Snow-White lay there in the coffin a long, long time, and she did not decay, but looked like she was asleep, for she was still as white as snow and as red as blood, and as black-haired as ebony wood.

Chapter 14: The Sleep of Death

When the dwarfs came home that evening,
they found Snow-White lying on the
ground. She was not breathing at all. She
was dead.
They lifted her up and looked for something
poisonous.
They undid her laces. They combed her
hair.
They washed her with water and wine. But
nothing helped.
The dear child was dead, and she remained
dead.

San Juan de la Cruz was a Christian mystic who lived in the latter part of the 16th century. He is remembered as an esteemed saint of the church who summarized and epitomized Spanish theological/philosophical thought. The western world remembers him as St. John of the Cross, and his work is still read and studied in virtually every seminary in the world, both Catholic and Protestant.

One of his poems describes a journey that has since been dubbed "The Dark Night of the Soul." In it he describes a mental and spiritual darkness that can overcome us from time to time, rendering us practically immobile. We feel totally cut off and despondent. Nothing makes sense. God, if God exists at all, seems completely separate and even foreign. Life seems hopeless. There is no light to be found in a long night of spiritual darkness. It is as if we are mentally and spiritually dead, but our body, for whatever reason, lives on.

The great mystic Eckhart Tolle was asked about his own experience of trying to endure one of these episodes. He answered the question on his website. This is a paraphrase of that response:

The "dark night of the soul" is a term that goes back a long time. Yes, I have experienced it. It is a term used to describe what one could call a collapse of perceived meaning in life … an eruption into your life of a deep sense of meaninglessness. The inner state in some cases is very close to what is conventionally called depression. Nothing makes sense anymore. There's no purpose to anything.

That results in a dark place.

If you have ever experienced something like this, you well know that it consists of a depression so deep that it feels like death. It's as though you will never experience joy again. For all practical purposes, the only thing that will relieve your suffering appears to be physical death.

Your friends try to help. They metaphorically "*lift you up and look for something poisonous.*" They give you what they hope is good advice and point out your shortcomings. They try to tell you they understand what you are feeling, because something similar once happened to them.

They "*undo your laces, comb your hair,*" and even "*wash you with water and wine,*" or sometimes just wine. All this well-intentioned effort is supposed to make you feel better. "*But nothing helps.*" You are as good as dead. "*And [you] remain dead.*"

Nothing interests you. You lose all ability to function. Simply getting up in the morning, assuming you slept at all during the night, takes more effort than you can muster. A heavy, heavy weight feels piled on your shoulders, and facing a new day appears utterly impossible.

Queen Ego has seemingly defeated you. Everything you took pride in, everything that once gave you a reason to be happy, has been poisoned. The depression may have resulted from the death of someone close to you or a horrible loss of some kind. But the end result feels very close to spiritual death.

Thus it was for Snow-White. Her dwarf friends could do nothing except go through the motions. They tried. Oh, how they tried. But there was nothing they could really do. So they mourned for her in the only way they could.

They laid her on a bier, and all seven sat
next to her and mourned for her
and cried for three days.

They were going to bury her, but she still

looked as fresh as a living person, and still

had her beautiful red cheeks.

They said, "We cannot bury her in the

black earth,"

and they had a transparent glass coffin

made, so she could be seen from all sides.

They laid her inside, and with golden

letters wrote on it her name,

and that she was a princess.

Then they put the coffin outside on a

mountain, and one of them always stayed

with it and watched over her.

What do you do when your soul appears to have died? How do you react?

Primal Soul lives in the land of spirituality. When many people say the word spirituality, they immediately think of the word religion. But spirituality is not remotely the same thing as religion. As a matter of fact, it is easy to make the case that religion is often nothing more than "*a transparent glass coffin*," made to exhibit something that was once vibrantly alive and pulsing with life. Inside the coffin lies the body of Primal Soul, remembered as the princess she once was.

Jesus is credited with saying much the same thing in Matthew 23:27 in the New Testament:

"What sorrow awaits you teachers of religious law. Hypocrites! For you are like whitewashed tombs—beautiful on the outside but filled on the inside with dead people's bones and all sorts of impurity."

Every world religion in existence today, with one exception, began because someone, a Founder, had a spiritual vision of a better way to live. The only exception is the family of religions often lumped together under the name *Hinduism,* which didn't have just one Founder. They had many. The Founders were in contact with something "other," something higher, something beautiful. They experienced their transcendent Primal Soul. It had been born into the material world, evolved in nature, and developed within a universe of infinite possibilities. The Founders sought to free human beings from the confines of space and time. They attempted to lift our eyes upward toward heaven, and conceived of eternity and infinity in a moment of time.

Their initial vision was often sufficient to inspire a group of followers to experience, if only for a minute, a transforming vision. Those disciples may have not been able to hold on to it. They may have been *Keepers* of the Sacred Flame rather than *Bearers* of it within their hearts and minds. But they recognized the vision for what it was, and carried it forward after the Founder was gone.

Generation after generation, followers diluted the original inspiration. Primal Soul, once at the center of the action, and the generating source of human spirituality, slowly began to die. The Keepers of the Sacred Flame often lost their focus. Those who once shepherded a transforming vision became, first, museum curators, and then prison guards. Spiritual freedom morphed into religious dogma and doctrinal custom.

Those who came later didn't completely bury Primal Soul "*in the black earth.*" They did something much worse. They enshrined her in glass cathedrals and magnificent edifices of stone and marble. They surrounded her with ritual and artistic expressions. They lauded her even as they oversaw her demise and watched over her death. They entombed spirituality in the coffin of religion.

Look at what passes for spirituality in much of the religious world today. To prove this point, we don't have to bring up obvious evils such as clergy child-abuse scandals, involving no less that thousands of those who masqueraded as Keepers of the Sacred Flame but instead wore the black cloaks of an evil, power-hungry lust. We don't even have to mention those who attempted to highjack religious institutions so as to turn them into political machines. We don't have to talk about so-called media evangelists who preach a thinly disguised materialistic "gospel" of wealth and prosperity, let alone those who, in the name of their God, go forth to misguided and destructive war.

No, we can observe the display of dead spirituality much closer to home on a smaller, but just as obvious, scale. We can see it in the vacant faces of those who pay lip-service to spirit by reciting ostentatious prayers in front of those who hypocritically bow their heads, close their eyes, and think irrelevant thoughts.

We can see Primal Soul on display in her coffin when we observe "religious" people of God who attend worship services one day a week and flagrantly exploit their communities on the other six by engaging in practices that promote wealth over well-being.

The Jewish Rabbi-turned-Christian-apostle Paul, himself a very flawed Keeper of the Sacred Flame, saw it coming a mile away. Even before Christianity became institutionalized, he ranted against trends he already saw developing in his religious community. In II Timothy 3:6, he warned against those who had an "outward form of godliness" but denied its power. "Turn away from such as these," he cried.

A glass coffin of institutional religion may be beautiful. It may display the spirituality of Primal Soul for all to view from a discreet distance. Its followers may place it "*on a mountain*" for all to see and constantly "*stay with it and watch over it.*" But religion such as this is still a coffin. Its purpose is to house the dead. The "*golden letters*" that declare the contents of the coffin to be royal—"*a princess*"—are still the inscription on a tombstone, no matter how gilded and splendid their outward appearance.

Religion isn't evil. At its best it offers community, spiritual aid and instruction, a grounding experience, and eternal hope. But when it becomes a coffin that houses a dead spirituality, it has failed, no matter how elegant its ritual.

The animals too came and mourned for
Snow-white,
first an owl, then a raven, and finally a
dove.

At this point of the narrative, we are offered a ray of hope. We return to the motif of nature. Except for a representative of the Keepers of the Sacred Flame, who stood guard at Snow-White's tomb, people didn't come and mourn. But nature's residents did. One by one, the animals come to pay homage.

We are thus given a hint that the story may not yet be over. Something seems to be stirring, especially when we consider the symbolic meaning behind the visitors. If Snow-White's "redemption draweth nigh," to again quote the Bible, nature itself may prove to be her salvation.

For the metaphorical significance of the specific birds that now enter our story, we turn to the work of Ted Andrews, who is a student of symbolism and spirituality in nature. In his book, *Animal Speak*, he revealed the universal message brought by each of the three visitors who came to pay homage to Primal Soul.

• Owl represents the gift of the spirit of power. This messenger asks us to pay attention to dreams and visions which open a window to the world of spirituality. Although it is up to us to act on that power, the opportunity is always present.

• Raven is a shape shifter. Its presence indicates that things are changing around us. Magic is awakening. Our job is to give it expression in order to change our lives for the better.

• Dove tells us that a new cycle of opportunity is at hand. A time of peace and prosperity may well be in our future. We need to mourn, yes, but we then need to release our emotions, guilt, fears and anxieties. New birth is at hand.

When any of these gift-givers appear in our lives, they bring with them a wake-up call. Even in the sleep of death we are never without hope. Remember that Primal Soul, though it may appear dead and gone, is eternal. All we have to do is hang on. Miracles happen. The key to getting through a very real dark night of the soul is found in the word, "through." It may seem like forever, but it's always darkest just before the dawn.

Snow-White lay there in the coffin a long,
long time, and she did not decay,
but looked like she was asleep, for she was
still as white as snow
and as red as blood,
and as black-haired as ebony wood.

Only now, finally, as the story reaches its climax, do we learn something very important, something the author had, until now, kept secret from us.

Earlier we were told that the child was "*black as ebony wood*," but what that meant was never exactly divulged. The only "black" reference was the window frame through which Queen Ego looked out on the earth. We were forced to come to our own conclusions, simply filing away the reference without really understanding what was meant by it.

Only now do we learn the truth. Black was the color of Snow-White's hair, the capstone of Primal Soul's glory, and, most importantly, the source of pride that almost brought about her downfall by way of a poisoned comb.

Why did we have to wait so long to find this out? Why wait until now to disclose something this significant?

Maybe this is the reason: We learn only now that Snow-White's hair was black because the author didn't want to cast an as yet unearned shadow over Primal Soul—the very shadow under which we all live. In other words, until Snow-White made her intentional choice and brought about a specific event, the metaphorical color black was only a possibility. It didn't necessarily have to come to pass in her reality.

Now it becomes obvious. Besides being the color of the frame through which Queen Ego viewed life "out there" in nature, the color black also represents possibilities that are constantly before and above us, dependent upon our choices. Those choices are the crowning glory of life and the reason we are born in the first place. But nothing is manifested until we choose to make it so. Both good and bad burst into fruition only through our intention. We are the center of our life's story, and its primary author. Our metaphorical hair may be black, it may be red, it may be blond. We won't find out until we choose our path.

Snow-White didn't have to make the choice she did. She could have shut the door, followed the advice of the Keepers of the Sacred Flame, and escaped all this unpleasantness.

So can we. Our futures are not set in stone. Yes, we live our lives with black hair over our heads, symbolizing a cloud of possibilities that might or might not come to pass. One of them is the possibility that we might bring about our own ruin. But whether or not we do so is up to us. We don't have to eagerly reach for the poison comb, and we don't have to eat the tempting apple. We don't have to buy Ego's wares.

Once again, we turn to the words of the immortal Bard. "It is not in the stars to hold our destiny, but in ourselves," said Shakespeare, through his hero Julius Caesar.

Let's be as succinct as possible. Like the "death-or-life" question posed by Schrodinger's famous proverbial cat, the color of Snow-White's hair was not revealed to us until she made her choice. Only then did we come to learn the truth that haunted her life from the beginning. "*White as snow, red as blood, black as ebony wood*!" Anything had been possible. Any color could have been manifested. But with her choice, only one condensed into reality. So now all three lay supposedly dead in a coffin, a victim of pathological ego. We are left with one reality and an infinite number of questions concerning "what might have been."

In the same way, we do not know the outcome of our own choices. Every day offers a clean slate—both yin and yang. In this world of dualism, at every fork in the road we are offered a choice. We have no idea what the outcome of that choice might be. The best we can do is be aware of ego's wiles, and follow our hearts.

That is the purpose of this story. That is the message the author wants to convey. That is the central teaching in the story of Snow-White.

At this point it is probably best if you take a short break and meditate for a few moments about the choices you have made so far throughout your life. Some were undoubtedly good ones.

The ones you remember most vividly, however, will probably be the ones that produced questionable outcomes. Perhaps you might even find yourself right now experiencing a dark night of the soul. Your choices might have conspired to make it appear as if you are in a spiritual black hole that seems to offer no hope. Perhaps you are facing what appears to be the sleep of death.

If so, read on. There is a path that leads through the dark night. Healing is possible. We are about to discover that nature itself is on our side. We have only to align ourselves with its blessings. Sleep does not last forever. It's time to awaken from your dream.

THE TEXT

Now it came to pass that a prince entered these woods and happened onto the dwarfs' house, where he sought shelter for the night. He saw the coffin on the mountain with beautiful Snow-White in it, and he read what was written on it with golden letters.

Then he said to the dwarfs, "Let me have the coffin. I will give you anything you want for it."

But the dwarfs answered, "We will not sell it for all the gold in the world."

Then he said, "Then give it to me, for I cannot live without being able to see Snow-White. I will honor her and respect her as my most cherished one."

As he thus spoke, the good dwarfs felt pity for him and gave him the coffin. The prince had his servants carry it away on their shoulders. But then it happened that *one of them stumbled on some brush, and this dislodged from Snow-White's throat the piece of poisoned apple that she had bitten off. Not long afterward she opened her eyes, lifted the lid from her coffin, sat up, and was alive again.*

Chapter 15: The Healing Power of Earth Energies

Now it came to pass that a prince entered these woods and happened onto the dwarfs' house, where he sought shelter for the night.
He saw the coffin on the mountain with beautiful Snow-White in it,
and he read what was written on it with golden letters.
Then he said to the dwarfs,
"Let me have the coffin. I will give you anything you want for it."
But the dwarfs answered,
"We will not sell it for all the gold in the world."
Then he said,
"Then give it to me, for I cannot live without being able to see Snow-White.
I will honor her and respect her as my most cherished one."

The story of *Little Snow-White* has been told for a very long time. It has certainly evolved over the years. Some changes were probably for the good. Others border on blasphemy.

Of the latter group, the one that undoubtedly made the original story-tellers turn over in their graves was the 1937 version made into the world's first full-length animated film by Walt Disney. In terms of music, art, and technology, that film was brilliant. As a period piece, operating within the social norms of its day, it was somewhat acceptable, even though hindsight causes us to raise our eyebrows. But when it comes to completely obliterating the original intent of the story, it was nothing short of an abomination. In one short, cinematic sequence, the Disney version completely undermined the whole point of the tale and glorified the very patriarchy the original story meant to expose.

In the film version, the handsome prince "rescues" the helpless, sleeping, princess with a kiss. Talk about enforcing social stereotypes! Without even getting into the whole kissing-a-drugged-woman thing, which is bad enough in and of itself, everyone who saw that film, young and old, was inoculated against the whole intent of the story.

There are very few people alive today who realize that in the original version of the tale, the prince had very little to do with Snow-White's recovery from the sleep of death. In my conversations, as I have discovered in the course of writing about it, if we even mention Snow-White to someone, that famous kiss is so embedded in our cultural brains that the story's message becomes entirely lost on us.

No wonder it has become a "mere" fairy story. On that basis alone, it is impossible to imagine the harm Walt Disney has done to a society that needs to understand the message of this story more now than at any time in the history of our culture.

If you have come under the psychological influence of the film version, please do your best to get it out of your head and approach its central message with fresh eyes and ears. It will be to your benefit to do so.

We'll save the supposed kiss for a minute, and first seek to understand the identity of the prince.

Snow-White is a princess in that she is the daughter of a queen. As such, her male counterpart is a prince from an unnamed, unknown country. He was obviously on unfamiliar ground because he sought shelter at the home of the dwarfs, the Keepers of the Sacred Flame.

Of all the places available to him, why did he happen to choose this particular house? We are not told, but something must have beckoned him here, because the princess was initially attracted to the very same house and people. They both saw something unique about this particular place. It called to them in their need.

Nature does that sometimes. Why did our ancestors choose to build magnificent monuments of stone where we find them today? They are often found way off the beaten track at hard-to-reach locations. Why are certain geographical areas such as mountaintops or sacred springs visited by thousands of seekers every year? Because pilgrims are drawn to them, called by unseen earth energies.

Nature is magical. She continually seeks to revive her children.

This gives us our first clue. There is a nature-connection between the prince and the princess. Its source lies in the fact that they are both drawn by the same energetic force to the same location. There they recognize something unique and meaningful. They might not have recognized exactly what it was, but they both came under its influence.

That brings us to our second clue. There is another connection between the prince and the princess. When the prince sees the princess, he is attracted not only to her, but to her coffin, and the words written on it in gold.

Do you remember those words? They indicated her name and her position. Her name was Snow-White, which means Primal Soul. Her position was that of royal princess—or Intuitive Innocence, daughter of Spirit, eternal citizen of the Source. Her coffin, which symbolized religious, institutionalized spirituality, housed her remains.

Because I was a Christian pastor for many years, I saw this scene repeated almost every week. Someone experienced something in life that caused a spiritual awakening of some kind. They glimpsed the Holy. They didn't know what to do. Where could they go to discover more about their experience?

Their first instinct was usually to go to church. What did they find there? Sad to say, they often discovered only a kind of mummified version of what they were looking for.

They had seen a vibrant, spiritual vision. They found only a dead faith.

They had heard the metaphorical voice of angels. They discovered only sleepy and worn-out voices, accompanied by an off-key organ.

They sought the voice of God. They heard only announcements concerning an upcoming pot luck supper.

Even if their visit to church included magnificent spectacle and elaborate ritual performed by trained, professional clergy, no human tradition could encompass the embrace of the Holy. Of course human religion falls short. It has to. It is, after all, a human invention.

Never the less, the religious experience is better than nothing. "*Let me have the coffin. I will give you anything you want for it,*" said the prince, now identified as a Seeker from Beyond who is looking for the restoration of wholeness.

So great is our desire for spirituality that when our inner prince takes us to the mysterious land of the Source, seeking a restoration of unity within the human physical experience, we will pay for restoration with every pearl of great price we have at our disposal. No cost is too great. We want unity because it embodies that which we most desire. We will gladly give the whole world if we can only regain our soul.

But the price is beyond anything we possess. The dwarfs, those who keep the Sacred Flame, won't sell it for any amount. *"We will not sell it for all the gold in the world,"* they say.

"Then give it to me, for I cannot live without being able to see Snow-White. I will honor her and respect her as my most cherished one."

So great is our desire for unity with Primal Soul in authentic spirituality, our desire to regain our Intuitive Innocence, that we finally come to understand we can never purchase it. Primal Soul cannot be bought. It is already ours. It always was. And always will be.

That leads to our third point of connection between the prince and the princess. They are not *about* to be joined. They are *already* joined. And they always were. They are opposite poles of a spiritual Duality (notice the capitol "D") which transcends the earthly duality (with a lower case "d") of material existence.

The prince *is* the princess. The princess *is* the prince. They do not represent two separate genders and identities. They are above and beyond gender. Gender only manifests itself here in the material world. So even a journey from the Source into the material existence of human life cannot separate us from our essential identity. We are one with Spirit. Part of us, the essential, eternal part, remains behind. Temporary separation is merely an illusion. An important one, if we are to truly experience life in the material world of nature. But an illusion, just the same.

So when our spiritual prince enters the material world where our physical princess has taken on an earthly body in order to gain an experience of life, it is only natural that both are attracted to the same place.

And to each other. They are Soul mates.

As he thus spoke, the good dwarfs felt pity
for him and gave him the coffin.
The prince had his servants carry it away
on their shoulders.
But then it happened that one of them
stumbled on some brush, and this dislodged
from Snow-White's throat the piece of
poisoned apple that she had bitten off.
Not long afterward she opened her eyes,
lifted the lid from her coffin,
sat up, and was alive again.

It may seem as though the religions of the world display only the mummified corpse of a dead spirituality, supervised by a small group of devoted Keepers of the Sacred Flame, who hope against hope that the spirituality under their care still lives on, seemingly against all hope. But the sacred, beating heart of the Primal Soul they guard is not dead. When the Seeker from Beyond, looking for the restoration of wholeness, comes to claim that which is his, and which has always been his, the miracle comes to pass. Snow-White rises from the dead. "*Not long afterward she opened her eyes, lifted the lid from her coffin, sat up, and was alive again."*

How did it happen? What restored her life? Was it a kiss from a charming prince? Was she rescued by human love or lust?

No! Snow-White was brought back to life when Nature herself reached out to her. One of the bearers *"stumbled on some brush, and this dislodged from Snow-White's throat the piece of poisoned apple that she had bitten off."*

At the very beginning of our story, Snow-White was born into a natural world where *"snowflakes fell like feathers from heaven."* The natural world is our Earth Mother. Queen Ego is only our step mother.

Ego believes Primal Soul is her creation, but she did not give birth to us. Our earthly lives were conceived in Mother Nature's womb, and we evolved within her embrace. In our hour of need, it is the Earth itself who will restore us to life. Her minions will reach out, shake us up, dislodge the poison apple from where it is stuck in our throats, and revive our souls.

Our religions do not need to become coffins or museums, displaying only the dead or dying remains of spirituality. They need to return to the natural world from whence they sprang. They need to reconnect us with our Earth Mother. Only her healing powers can save us.

Now the central meaning of this story becomes clear. It is a tale that deals with earth energies that create and sustain material existence. Snow-White was born of such energies. The huntsman personified them, without fully grasping their beauty. The dwarfs lived and worked deep in their embrace.

But Ego poisoned the Earth Mother's creation, and it brought down her loveliest child.

Likewise, we are, even as you read these words, doing the exact same thing to Mother Earth. Our egos have sought to wrest what we mistakenly call the "good life" from our mother's bosom, and we are choking on our own misdeeds. The environmental headlines reveal the ugly truth. In our greed and contempt, we have heard the siren call of Queen Ego, and poisoned our nest.

The creative and restorative forces of earth energy are embedded within every fiber of nature. They are visible from the migration patterns of birds and butterflies to the latest research results stemming from the search for the Higgs Boson particle (the so-called "God" particle) currently under investigation at the Large Hadron Collider in the European particle laboratory at CERN.

But our civilization has turned its back on earth energy, and it is killing our souls. Once upon a time, our ancestors, being as much a product of earth energy as birds and butterflies, and while living much closer to nature than we do, recognized the effect these energies had upon them. They invented names such as spirits, fairies, gnomes, trolls, and even gods. As we have seen, religions always form around initial visions, so from these early beliefs inevitably developed the world's first religion, Animism.

The rise of ego, inspired by relentlessly left-brain, analytical methods of thought, cast much of this ancient religion aside. We began to call it mythology and superstition. But the underlying force of earth energies continued to manifest their existence to those who were attuned to the old ways.

Australian Aborigine elders still claim to see a landscape seamed with energy lines. Modern contractors in

Hawaii, even in this day and age, make it a practice to consult with Kahunas before orienting new buildings. New York businesses sometimes hire Feng Shui masters to design office spaces. Many well drillers will not move their equipment into position until a sensitive old-timer surveys the area with dowsing rods or a forked willow branch. Police departments quietly employ dowsers who search for lost people with a high-resolution topographical map and a swinging pendulum.

In short, the phenomenon of earth energy is still with us. How could it be otherwise? It gave us birth. We may have become prodigal children who seek our own way in life, thinking we know better. But mothers always love their children. It's time for humanity to wake up from the death of sleep, and come home. We need to enter a new phase of existence. We need to be jolted awake into a new understanding and practice of earth magic. Sleepers, awake!

In our day and age, the Seeker from Beyond seems to be stuck with the coffin of organized religion. There is no doubt about the statistics. Attendance at all religious institutions is down. Christian churches are closing by the hundreds each year. Jews differentiate between secular and sacred wings of their tradition. If you say the word "Islamic" in most conversations, the next word to follow is often associated with "terrorist."

But people still claim to be spiritual. A healthy majority of people report that they have experienced a transforming moment with their God.

Steven D. Smith, in his book *Pagans and Christians in the City: Culture Wars From the Tiber to the Potomac*, puts forth the thesis that what appears to be encroaching secularism is, in fact, an illusion. He believes that modern culture is experiencing a rebirth of pagan religion, or Animism. It was thought to be dead and buried by the Christian Church, who burned much of it at the stake and declared it to be heretical.

What they couldn't destroy, such as popular Christmas and Easter traditions, they baptized, and called their own. But according to Smith, it wasn't dead after all. It was just placed in a coffin and put on display. And now it's reawakening with new language and modern conceptualizations that are more palatable to today's believers.

In short, people are beginning to recognize a divinity *within* the natural world, rather than *outside* it. "God" is to be found "in here," rather than "out there." Metaphysical experiences are not just transcendent, they are imminent.

Mother Nature has reached out and tripped up those who bear the coffin. The poisonous fruit that rendered us immobile and brought on what appeared to be a sleep of death is even now being dislodged from our throats and we are coming alive.

The big question is this: Is it too late?

THE TEXT

"Good heavens, where am I?" she cried out.

The prince said joyfully, "You are with me."

He told her what had happened, and then said, "I love you more than anything else in the world. Come with me to my father's castle. You shall become my wife."

Snow-White loved him, and she went with him.

Their wedding was planned with great splendor and majesty.

Chapter 16: Reunion

"Good heavens, where am I?" she cried
out.
The prince said joyfully, "You are with
me."
He told her what had happened, and then
said,
"I love you more than anything else in the
world. Come with me to my father's castle.
You shall become my wife."

I t's time now to examine in more detail the relationship between the princess and the prince. It lies at the very heart of our story. Indeed, *Little Snow-White* cannot be fully understood without understanding that relationship. But in doing so, we come to some cultural problems.

First off, we have been taught since we were children that man/woman gender issues are central, especially in supposed "fairy tales for children." Little girls grow up to be beautiful princesses. Little boys grow up to be charming princes. Both, we are told, should exhibit socially accepted rules and attributes of their gender.

When the royal wedding took place in London, we often heard the expression, "fairy tale wedding." As a minister I often participated in weddings designed to make the bride look, and be treated, as a "princess." It's hard to avoid, no matter how hard we try.

But we are trying. At many Christian church weddings, it is customary to place a single, unlit candle on the altar during the service, flanked by two lit candles. The two candles symbolize the bride and groom. At the end of the service, the new couple steps forward and lights the center candle. It's a potent symbol which illustrates the words, "The two shall become one."

In the past it was often traditional that the two would then blow out their own candles, signifying the creation of a single entity from two individual people. More and more, however, the current custom is to leave all three candles burning. This changes the symbolism. The meaning now is that they have created something new—their marriage—while retaining their individuality.

This custom is much closer to the imagery of cultural acceptance being more and more practiced today, at least in western countries.

Little-Snow White, however, transcends even this imagery. It takes us back to the place where male and female were one, before the journey into material life required the split into two genders. The process of spiritual evolution is a mechanism through which we move from innocent unity, as experienced by Snow-White, through an agonizing experience of separation and heartache, even death, to the point where we return to mature unity, as evidenced by the reunion of prince and princess. Snow-White now understands perfectly well the journey she has undergone. And she understands where her identity really lies. "*Good heavens, where am I?*" *she cried out.* Confused, she addresses her question to her true home, heaven.

The prince, her other half, is able to explain the nature of her journey, and that she has now returned to the Source. Her adventure is complete, her mission into material life accomplished. It's time to go home. "*The prince said joyfully, 'You are with me.' He told her what had happened.*"

With normal human cultural lenses solidly in place, it's difficult to view the prince and princess characters in *Little Snow-White* in any other than a traditional light. The charming prince rescues the beautiful princess. They get married and live happily ever after. What else is there to say?

But the original intent of this story was not at all like that. It transcends gender altogether. We understand men and women in terms of sex because we live in a dualistic culture that often can't get past the opposite polar dimensions of life in a material world. When life is manifested in the reality apparent to our five senses, it splits into two genders. We associate certain attributes with each one, and a dichotomy is the result.

This in spite of the fact that we all know women often demonstrate male attributes, and men demonstrate feminine attributes. Both are present in each of us. Traditionally, however, we are taught at an early age to discourage the public display of such differences. A young, athletic girl is a "tomboy." "Boys shouldn't cry." We've all heard those sentiments expressed.

What we see in the story of *Little Snow-White* is a reunion of transcendent unity—the eternal unity that precedes life on earth.

Let's try to put it in the simplest terms possible. Stick with me as we conduct a thought experiment, trying to put in basic language what the journey from the Source to life might look like.

Please be warned in advance that this is strictly my own understanding. I make no claim to divine understanding or insight. But it helps me to make sense of the mystery of life, so I put it forth with the hope that it might help you. What follows is only a mental construct. It's probably simplistic. But it might serve as a good place to start. I've tried, over the years, to arrive at a visual representation that merges theology, philosophy, metaphysics, and science. This might not prove to be the ultimate answer, so remember that it's only meant to serve as a metaphor. Don't get too literal with it.

Let's begin at the place I call the Source, the place everything begins. What is it?

The truth is, no one knows. Traditionally we call it God, but that name has so much baggage attached to it these days that some people might not be comfortable with it. You might prefer something else, such as Great Mystery, Higher Power, or Ultimate Unknown. In India, it's Brahman. The Indians of New England called it Kitchi Manitou. Others used the term Great Spirit. Call it what you will, but for our purposes, we'll call it the Source.

Picture the person characterized in our story by Snow-White as a wave of some kind of energy within that Source. She has no shape or form. She takes up no space but she contains infinite possibility. She travels at no speed and exists in perfect rest but has infinite potential.

Along with her in the Source are an infinite number of other waves. But that fact isn't really apparent because all waves are one wave. She isn't anything approaching individuality, because all is One. Her story hasn't yet begun.

Before the story begins, prince, princess, and every other character in the drama are united with all things in a single whole. But they cannot grow and personally develop through such a unity. The only way to do so is to develop uniqueness. And the only way to do that is through individual experience.

One day, if we can allow even the concept of something called a "day," it happened that a single wave broke out and began its journey towards uniqueness— towards individuality and singular experience. This wave would soon be called Snow-White.

This will eventually happen with every wave. When they all undergo such transformation, each on its own journey, total potentiality will have become possible. All that is required is space and time, and eventually every single possible experience will become realized. When all such waves finally complete their story and unite back home, the Source will then have become—and will have personally experienced—everything. Every potentiality will have been realized. The Source will have become infinite, realized possibility. All the individual stories will have become one story.

Whatever the Source is, religions all over the world speculate that love is at the center of existence. We might even say that the Source itself is love. The Bible, and many other holy books, agree that "God is love" (I John 4:8). So of course, the story of *Little Snow-White* is a love story. That's what all stories are, eventually. Love makes the world go 'round.

But here is where the prince and princess, united in perfect love, begin the process of separation. One will eventually be born in human form and become Snow-White. The other will remain behind in the Source. But they will forever be spiritually entangled. They will always be connected.

Eventually both will enter our story and become united in material life, as they once were in the Source, the dimension of spirit. But they have a long journey to make before this is realized. First, they must experience the problems inherent in their separation. As the princess is about to learn the hard way, *realized* possibilities are not always *nice* possibilities. To put it simply, potentiality has a downside. Good and bad, yin and yang. Pairs of opposites now enter the picture.

This is where things get interesting.

In evolutionary terms here on earth, we cannot become emotionally mature as adults without experiencing the pain of separation from first our mother and then our family. There is no other way to grow. This is illustrated in the tale of *Little Snow-White*. The princess had to experience separateness. Even the separateness of death. It's all part of the process of life.

Returning to our metaphor, when the wave of potential that became Snow-White was safely ensconced in the Source, when she began her journey and moved "out," if we can use that expression, her story began. She moved out. But "out" into what? Where did she first find herself? What environment did she inhabit?

I like to use the word Consciousness. It is what both Albert Einstein and Stephen Hawking once called "The Mind of God."

Although she still had no mass, either physical or metaphysical, her story at least began to take on weight and substance. She hadn't yet visualized where she was going, or what she would look like, but she somehow became aware that eventually she would.

The "Mind of God" is an interesting place. It corresponds, in the story of *Little Snow-White,* to the original author of this story beginning to conceive of what might come next. The telling of the story is the act of creation. What might happen? How will this story differ from any other story? What lessons might be learned? What does it feel like to be alone, for instance? What is it like to face death? How does it feel to meet new and different friends and allies?

There is only one way to find out. That way is forward.

The princess now entered her first defining field. It was a place wherein she began to take on shape. Not mass. Not yet. But she grew a little "heavier" as she began to transform herself into something truly unique and separate. Ideas formed and morphed into new possibilities. This is the yeasty field of creativity.

Taking a cue from the ancient Hindus, I call this place of transformation the Akashic Field. Everything that we know and experience around us, every rock, tree, and flower, every person, was first conceived in Akasha. From the standpoint of life on earth, here's where the story really begins

Plato once made it a point to differentiate between what he called "horse" from the concept of "horseness." "Horseness" is the eternal reality. The "horse" quietly grazing on clover in the pasture by the side of the road is just its physical manifestation.

A "horse" doesn't exist in the Akashic Field. But this is where "horseness" dwells. Snow-White hadn't yet been born as a human. But she was now conceived.

The Akashic Field is the place in which uniqueness is first demonstrated. There is not yet a Snow-White, but such a possibility now becomes concrete. We who read the story come to understand that unique individuality can lead to unique experience. There is now some direction. "*If only I had a child as white as snow, as red as blood, and as black as the wood in this frame.*" A field of snow, a drop of blood, and a wish for a child. What's next?

A theoretical physicist reading this story might think of the princess as existing in the world of Quantum reality. This world was discovered by our scientists only about a hundred years ago. We are just now beginning to explore it.

Sir James Hopwood Jeans, who died in 1946, was the first to visualize the universe as being more like a great thought than a great machine. So another way to conceive Quantum Reality might be to think in terms of a field of thoughts and intentions.

Snow-White wasn't a reality yet. She still had a way to go. All she was, you might say, was a wish. But she could now form an intention to enter into life and fulfill that wish.

Quantum Reality is a place of potential. We ego-driven, self-centered humans don't really sense its presence. But what Plato might have called "humanness" exists there, in potential. That potential is realized when we take one more step. In order for "humanness" to become "a human," Snow-White had to first "collapse" into the environment humans experience. To do that she had to pass through the newly discovered Higgs Field.

Physicists are universally excited that the existence of the Higgs Field has now been proved by experimental method. But ask them to describe that field, now that they know it's there, and they begin to get a little edgy.

It's a reality. That's for sure. But no one quite knows how to explain it. Let me share an example. Here is the simplest definition I could find, from Andrew Zimmerman Jones:

The Higgs field is the theoretical field of energy that permeates the universe, according to the theory put forth in 1964 by Scottish theoretical physicist Peter Higgs. Higgs suggested the field as a possible explanation for how the fundamental particles of the universe came to have mass, because in the 1960s the Standard Model of quantum physics actually couldn't explain the reason for mass itself. He proposed that this field existed throughout all of space and that particles gained their mass by interacting with it.

(http://physics.about.com/od/quantumphysics/f/HiggsFiel d.htm)

There are a lot of other definitions, but most of them involve some pretty complex mathematics. Suffice it to say that when energy passes through the Higgs Field, it emerges on our side with mass. In other words, it becomes material. It is now within our perception realm. The princess of our story was now Snow-White.

She exists in the world of our five senses. She's in the material realm. That's the world we see around us.

But don't forget the prince in all this, because he, too, is perfect love. Within the allegory of this story, he is forever entangled with the princess. Thus, he seeks her out, following in her wake until he finds her, and is reunited.

Snow-White loved him, and she went with him.
Their wedding was planned with great splendor and majesty.

This is not a story of one character "rescuing" another. This is a story about love triumphing even over death. Love, like Intuitive Innocence, or Primal Soul, is eternal. Nothing can separate or divide love, not even a journey through the Higgs Field, and the experiences of life on the other side. Real love is all about unity.

Ego, of course, doesn't realize this. Ego is concerned only about itself. So as the story continues, it's no surprise that we find ourselves gazing at another duality. Prince and princess are now united, facing a glorious reunion and a return to the eternal "*castle*" at the Source of everything that is.

Ego, on the other hand, stands again at her mirror, contemplating only herself.

THE TEXT

Snow-White's godless mother was also invited to the feast. After putting on her beautiful clothes she stepped before her mirror and said: "Mirror, mirror, on the wall, who in this land is fairest of all?"

The mirror answered: "You, my queen, are fair; it is true. But the young queen is a thousand times fairer than you."

The wicked woman uttered a curse, and she became so frightened, so frightened, that she did not know what to do. At first, she did not want to go to the wedding, but she found no peace. She had to go and see the young queen.

Chapter 17: Fear

Snow-White's godless mother was also
invited to the feast.
After putting on her beautiful clothes she
stepped before her mirror and said:
"Mirror, mirror, on the wall, who in this
land is fairest of all?"
The mirror answered: "You, my queen, are
fair; it is true.
But the young queen is a thousand times
fairer than you."
The wicked woman uttered a curse, and she
became so frightened, so frightened, that
she did not know what to do.

E go is all about fear. Fear permeates the very atmosphere ego breathes, and transforms every hour of life ego lives on earth. We usually are not aware of its shadow, because we start learning how to live with fear at a very young age. But love doesn't make ego's world go 'round. Fear does.

Try a thought experiment. Think of the number of times your language betrays the prevalence of fear in your life. Since ego personifies the word "I," think about the number of times the word "I," or ego, is paired with the word fear:

- "I'm afraid you're wrong."

- "I fear I'm doing the wrong thing."

- "I'm afraid that idea won't work."

- "I fear I'm coming down with something."

- "I'm afraid I won't be able to make it."

- "I fear for our future."

You can think of many more examples, I'm sure. "I'm afraid..." "I fear..." That kind of revelatory language permeates our speech because "I," ego, is suffused with fear. As we get older, we learn to live with it. Our childhood fearlessness slowly erodes away and we become inured to the feeling of fear. But fear is a constant companion throughout life.

When I used to teach biblical theology, I enjoyed pointing out the first words the gospel accounts usually place on the tongue of Jesus after the resurrection. His friends should have been overjoyed to see him. According to everything they had been taught, he was now raised from the dead. They should have been rejoicing. But what were the first words he said, time and time again? "Fear not!" When confronted with the unexpected or unknown, our first reaction is usually fear.

Life can be explained in many different ways, but one insightful description is that life is a constant battle to control and overcome fear. Even in the midst of our best moments, we are afraid they won't last. We spend whole portions of our days waiting for the other shoe to drop.

The marketing industry has learned this lesson very well. Its main technique is to make us afraid of something, so it can sell us a product that will help alleviate our fear.

A few years ago, I bought a new car. I made it plain to the saleswoman that my number one priority was reliability. Living out in the woods the way I do, it's difficult to get to a service station, and when I need a car, I generally need it to function smoothly.

"No problem," I was told, as she handed out statistical information proving that this particular car was the most reliable car on the road today. I was going to be able to drive this car for 300,000 miles or until I dropped dead, whichever came first. Considering the small number of miles I drive every year, it was pretty certain my car would outlive me. I mean, I really don't expect to live for 103 years.

I bought the car and drove it home, figuring I now had one less thing to worry about.

Before a year passed, however, I started to get letters from the dealership. They wanted to me to extend my warrantee. Nothing was wrong with the car. I was entirely satisfied with it. But if something happened, they said, I might not be covered. I could be stranded on the highway, late at night. Some essential part might fail at a critical time, causing a horrible accident. I might have to face monumental repair bills somewhere down the road. They painted fearsome pictures of doom and gloom if I wasn't insured properly.

The very company that less than a year before had promised complete reliability now tried to frighten me into buying more warranty coverage. "Be afraid!" they said. "Be very afraid! Buy more insurance! Alleviate your fears!

Sleep better at night! Sign on the dotted line! Spending more money will make you feel better!"

We see the same thing with health insurance. I've been told any number of times that I'm only one heart attack away from financial disaster. I should be afraid my family will suffer if I don't purchase the right funeral plan. This or that might happen, or something else will certainly go wrong. Be afraid!

Motivational fear even infuses mundane areas of life. "What might happen," I am asked, "if I need to contact someone and I don't have the right cell phone, along with all the latest downloads and upgrades?"

I didn't buy my first cell phone until I was fifty-five years old. I'm amazed I managed to survive that long without one.

I'm even advised to be afraid of things I did in the distant path. Because I'm a product of my culture, I was raised eating white bread and bacon. It's a miracle I ever managed to run a marathon. If I had known I would live to be as old as I am, I'm afraid I would have taken much better care of myself.

Watch the orgiastic fever the weather forecasters whip up when a snowstorm is about to hit. A warning that five inches of snow might be coming will guarantee that every generator in a three-state radius gets sold. It will also empty the grocery store shelves. How did we ever used to survive before television and its advanced warning systems?

That's how the marketing industry thrives. It's a self-perpetuating feed-back system that makes us afraid and then sells us something to deal with the fear it creates. And it all revolves around ego. How will "I" get by? What will happen to "me?" Remember, "I" and "me" are buzzwords for ego.

Our story now returns to Queen Ego herself, standing before her mirror.

Snow-White's godless mother was also invited to the feast. After putting on her beautiful clothes she stepped before her mirror and said:
"Mirror, mirror, on the wall, who in this land is fairest of all?

Notice how she is portrayed. She is now "*Snow-White's godless mother.*" As we have discovered, Snow-White was nature's child. She was about to be reunited with the Seeker from Beyond, her "self on the other side" of material reality, and Queen Ego just couldn't stay away from the party.

But the queen wanted to be the star of the show. Although she still considered Snow-White to be her daughter, Ego, as is always the case, wanted to be the center of attention. She put on her most beautiful dress, certain that every eye would be on her, and once again stood before her mirror, asking the same old question. This time, however, the response terrified her.

> *"You, my queen, are fair; it is true.*
> *But the young queen is a thousand times*
> *fairer than you."*

What was it about this particular response that caused the queen to be so afraid? Three times she had asked this question, and each time she had responded to the answer with a plot to murder Snow-White. Why was this time any different?

The answer is found in the mirror's response. Snow-White is no longer described as simply living "*beyond the mountains with the seven dwarfs.*" For the first time she is said to be "*the young queen.*"

Ego is finally brought face to face with the truth that, up until now, she has been unable to face. The princess is now revealed to be a queen. She has reunited with the prince, her spiritual counterpart.

Up to now, the Great Illusion had transpired to make the young queen, Primal Soul, forget for a while that she was eternal spirit. But having fulfilled her mission on earth, which was nothing less than the cumulative experiences of a lifetime lived in a physical body, she was now once again back in her proper place. She had awakened from sleep, pierced life's illusion, and realized that "life is but a dream."

No wonder Queen Ego was doubly frightened.

The wicked woman uttered a curse, and she
became
so frightened, so frightened,

320

that she did not know what to do.

With Primal Soul now preparing to return to the source, Ego no longer would have a body on which to fixate. For all practical purposes, Ego would cease to exist. Snow-White's eternal soul, having finished the work it came to earth to do, was about to return home. Ego's work, which should have been to nurture and care for Primal Soul, was done. There is only unity in the Source. Hence, there will be no further need for separate Ego. But rather than rejoice in a job well done, the now outsized Ego could not conceive of herself no longer existing—no longer needed. So she froze up with fear.

At first, she did not want to go to the
wedding, but she found no peace.
She had to go and see the young queen.

How do we keep our own egos in check? How do we live our lives with a healthy ego in place instead of allowing it to become pathological?

First of all, we need to recognize ego for what it is. Remember that it always tries to disguise itself. It makes itself very difficult to recognize.

None of us like to think we're a victim. We all want to believe we've got our egos under control. But how do we know for sure that a disguised ego isn't complicating our lives?

The answer is simple, but it's one we might find difficult to face.

Ask yourself a question. Are you afraid of something? If fear is at work in your life, chances are good that disguised ego is working in the dark somewhere. The way to measure how much our egos control us is to ask how afraid we are. The presence of fear always reveals ego's hold on us.

So the way forward doesn't revolve around identifying and controlling our ego. It involves casting out fear.

How do we do that? Can we really banish fear from our lives? Can we conquer our fears and become fearless once again?

Probably not. Any attempt to do so will undoubtedly be a lie. We might deceive ourselves for a while, pretending to push fear into the dark recesses of our minds, but we'll be kidding ourselves. Ego will have pulled off the greatest hoax of all. It will have disguised itself as its own conqueror.

There is only one way to defeat fear. We need to allow it no place to settle in. We do that by filling its environment with something else. It's an ancient wisdom, as old as the Bible, but perpetually true: "Perfect love casts out fear."

Think of it like this. Picture a container with grit and dirt at the bottom. The opening at the top is too small to allow you to reach inside and remove it, so what do you do?

The answer is simple. Fill the container with clean water. The dirt and grit will be carried to the surface. Once the container is filled to overflowing, it will float away with the rising tide.

You can't defeat negativity with more negativity. You can't fight ego with self-deception. You need positive energy. You need love. If your life is filled with love, ego will have no place to call its own.

If you are faced with a bully, or an ego-driven enemy, you won't defeat that enemy by "out-ego-ing" it. Your ego will feed your enemy's ego, and the returning hateful energy will fuel your own ego, and on and on it will spiral. Ego loves this self-perpetuating process. It's the loop that drives almost every institution that governs today's world.

As hard as it sounds, the only way to defeat ego, whose presence wears the disguise of fear, is by filling yourself with love.

Please follow what I'm saying here. Listen to the words but don't imitate my actions. I believe the truth of what I'm saying, but I can't do it very well. There are people in my life who I simply haven't been able to forgive, including myself. Some of them are old acquaintances. Many have been dead for years. There are quite a number of world leaders and politicians in the mix. A few are considered to be pillars of the church. Their negative energy feeds my negative energy. A force-field of negative energy grows and grows. And ego thrives on it.

What I mean by this confession is that filling yourself with perfect love is the answer to defeating ego, but it is a very, very difficult task.

Never the less, it is the only way. We probably can never achieve the goal. Maybe that's one of the lessons we need to learn from a lifetime on earth. Maybe perfect love is an ideal for which to strive rather than a goal to expect to achieve.

But doing the right thing cannot be measured by degree of difficulty.

The sad truth is that usually we not only *can't* forgive, we *don't want to*. There's something pervasive within us that almost enjoys hating our enemies. It gives us some kind of pathological comfort. That's why Queen Ego couldn't stay away from the wedding. Something within her told her she just had to be there, even though her evil had, in this case, been met with forgiveness.

Notice the text again: "*Snow-White's godless mother was also invited to the feast.*"

If anyone should have been excluded from the festivities, it should have been the old queen. But she was invited just the same. The invitation sent a powerful message. All could still be forgiven if ego would only return to her proper place. Love might yet transform even the one who chose murder and deceit over respect and encouragement. It wasn't yet too late. There was still a chance for reconciliation.

The choice was entirely up to the queen. How would her story end?

THE TEXT

When she arrived, she recognized Snow-White, and terrorized, she could only stand there without moving.

Then they put a pair of iron shoes into burning coals. They were brought forth with tongs and placed before her. She was forced to step into the red-hot shoes and dance until she fell down dead.

Chapter 18: Dancing Towards Destiny

When she arrived, she recognized Snow-
White, and terrorized, she could only stand
there without moving.

It's very difficult to change a life-long habit. As a lifetime member of the Worry-wart Association for the Glass-is-half-empty Society (WAGS) you can take my word for it on this one. My mother used to say to the young five-year-old who once occupied my body, "Jim, you worry too much!" She was right. And if she was still alive, she'd still be saying it.

That being said, I can identify with Queen Ego at this point in her story. Standing face to face with Primal Soul, who possessed by nature everything the old queen had coveted, and having recognized, only now at the end, her own shortcomings and failings, she could only "*stand there without moving*," paralyzed by fear.

Thousands of people who have engaged a near death experience tell us, over and over again, that one of the main features they remember is what has now been labeled a "life review." Thankfully, the experience is usually described as a helpful summation rather than a critical judgment. Apparently, it is designed as a way to underscore all the choices and resultant consequences of our actions throughout our life on earth. It seems to be a way to understand why things happened the way they did.

It was said of the Buddha that when he experienced enlightenment he understood, in a moment of time, how Karma had worked throughout his lives on earth. In a vision he saw all his previous incarnations and understood their connectedness, how they had brought him to this point in time and place. He sensed Karma at work—the guiding force that propels life forward. More important, in a sudden intuitive leap, he grasped how to break out of Samsara, the wheel of life, death, and rebirth. He had finally found that for which he had been searching, even though he hadn't known what he was looking for. He achieved the goal of his quest. Siddhartha became the Buddha, the Enlightened One. This made possible his final awakening

Buddhists like to tell the story of a man who one day happened upon the Buddha, who was meditating along the side of the road.

"Sir," the man said, "I can see that you are a holy man. Are you a god?"

"No," replied the Buddha. "I am not a god."

"Are you an angel, that you radiate such holiness?"

Again, the Buddha shook his head.

"Then what are you?" the man pleaded.

"I am awake," said the Buddha.

Snow-White had awakened from her dream. Queen Ego saw her as she truly was—an immortal princess— Primal Soul. And the queen was terrified. Her life flashed before her eyes. She must have seen, with horror, what she had done and what she had become. Paralyzed, all she could do was "*stand there without moving.*" The terrible truth was now fully revealed and there was no escaping it. She finally understood that Ego is mortal and its time on earth is limited to the span of a human lifetime. Only Soul lives forever. And there was nothing the old queen could do about it.

When we fear our own death, when we truthfully face that which we have, over the course of a lifetime, thought to be our mortal enemy, when the last, expensive, miracle of medical technology fails and the doctor delivers the verdict that has been the bane of our existence since we first drew breath, the human tendency is usually to recoil, as if we somehow failed some test. We're going to die. We're not going to live forever. Where did we go wrong?

I don't mean to make light of this feeling. As a minister who has stood at the bedside of hundreds of dying patients, I have often experienced the depths of despair that rise up to overwhelm even the people who think they prepared for that final moment.

But when a rising tide of fear floods our souls and drowns our perspective, it is a sure sign that ego is playing out her final end game. At the close, when she has nothing left to do, and has no further cards to be played in the game of life, she resorts to her final and best disguise—fear. It is precisely at this point we need to remember an essential lesson to be learned from this precious and important story.

Here's the message, in all its simplicity and power. Primal Soul lies under the magical protection of the Source itself. Intuitive Innocence is immortal and constantly seeks an experience of something new and engaging.

Furthermore, its quest goes on forever. Each lifetime is but another chapter in an eternal game of exciting exploration.

Fear not. In the words of an old, old psalmist, echoed by a master named Jesus some 1500 years later, "Know ye not that ye are gods?"

Your arm will not last forever. Your foot will not last forever. Your body will not last forever. Neither will your ego. They are all a part of material existence. They are all tethered to a mortal body, which is designed to carry out one purpose, and one purpose only: to offer your soul an experience of life in the material world. When that purpose has been fulfilled, you won't need your body anymore. Be glad when it happens, not fearful. It's a graduation ceremony, not a death sentence.

If only Queen Ego could have, even at the end, understood her true purpose. If only she could have acknowledged her rightful place and true identity.

But Ego is a creature of habit. She had coveted, envied, and pampered herself for too long. It was now an ingrained habit, which held her in thrall. Instead of rejoicing in her host's fulfillment, she was paralyzed with terror. Her greatest disguise, fear, had now become her only identity. She had played her part too well and identified with her body too closely. Now her end was certain.

But what a horrible way to die:

Then they put a pair of iron shoes into
burning coals.
They were brought forth with tongs and
placed before her.

This is the worst image in the whole story. No wonder the Disney people left it out of their movie. Send the kids out of the room. This part is not for children. It's not even for adults, if they want to banish terrible pictures from their heads. It depicts a terrible, inhuman, torture scene. What, in heaven's name, was the original author trying to tell us?

In fairness to whoever that author might have been, this is not the only morality play to end with a scene of horrible torture. The Jesus story, for instance, ends with a bloody crucifixion. Socrates was forced to drink poison. Julius Caesar was stabbed to death. Abraham Lincoln was shot. There are a lot of good stories that end terribly. This one is not unique. But it's still pretty gruesome.

She was forced to step into the red-hot shoes and dance until she fell down dead.

What possible meaning can we ascribe to such a terrible scene?

Let's start with the shoes. What do they represent?

Shoes anchor us to the earth. They support us. But they also separate us from our Earth Mother. This story began with Queen Ego separated from nature, looking out through a window with a frame "*as black as ebony wood.*" We end the story in the same manner.

The queen is now separated from nature by iron shoes. The only thing iron shoes are good for is to stomp and flatten. They don't allow any sensitivity. She couldn't possibly feel any earth energy through iron shoes. Especially ones that terribly seared her feet. To alleviate the pain of her separation all she could do was incessantly move—to dance and dance, until she dropped dead. The experience and pain of separation caused frantic activity that eventually killed her.

Dare I point out that we, too, live in an era of separation from nature, and the more we separate the more we fill our lives with frantic activity? Our technological age has slipped iron shoes, searing hot iron shoes, onto our feet and we are all dancing toward an unknown destiny.

The heat seems to be unbearable at times. What have we done to our fellow human beings? What have we done to our earth mother? How have we allowed such inept leadership in so many countries around the world? A perfect storm is arising around us. Its name is Ego. Armageddon doesn't appear to be only a metaphor anymore. Any number of things could destroy us. Technology, weather, war, overpopulation, disease, comets from on high, disillusionment, chemicals, economics, pollution—they all offer a gloomy picture of fast-approaching destruction.

And what do we do? We continue the dance of death. Nothing changes except the tempo. The frantic pace increases with each succeeding generation. Things are speeding up, not slowing down. It seems as though we just can't stop it. The human race, all of us, whether we like it or not, are dancing toward an unknown destiny. Like Queen Ego, we hear in our heads the incessant music of our own creation, and seemingly cannot stop until we dance to our doom.

But before we even consider the implications of our entire species, let's keep things at a personal level for a while longer.

It's really tempting to sit back at this point and decide that the queen got only what she deserved. It was right and proper that she was destroyed at the end. After all, she tried to kill off the princess three times. Why shouldn't we rejoice at her demise, awful death though it was?

Unfortunately, this attitude is nothing less than disguised ego, back from the dead. The cause for our feeling of triumph when we see evil violently destroyed is called The Myth of Redemptive Violence. That is the belief that we should rejoice when violence, justified by supposed righteous, triumphs in the end.

When I was young, the bad guys on TV never got killed. Gene Autry and Roy Rogers just shot the guns out of their hands. Then came John Wayne and his compadres, and things started to escalate. Even during the 70s, however, the "A-Team" could drive through a hail of bullets and bombs, blow up a van or two, and watch everybody walk away, shaken but still alive and fit to go to jail.

With the arrival of Clint Eastwood's spaghetti westerns, though, the die was cast. Bad guys died. Period.

Admit it. You cheered along with the rest of the theater when the Death Star exploded, didn't you? Served them right. There wasn't a single innocent person among Darth Vader's vast minions, was there? They all got what they deserved and we could all go home feeling righteous and justified.

To see how far the trend has progressed, take a look at your kid's latest video game. Young children today, and, for that matter, adults who watch police shows on TV, now experience more death and destruction in a single evening than I was exposed to in my entire youth. We justify it because we see it as somehow morally upright for bad guys to die within the context of the triumph of truth and justice.

That's the Myth of Redemptive Violence. Violence is okay, even entertaining, as long as it is used in the name of good.

It's hard to argue the point. Sometimes bad guys can only be stopped by good guys doing otherwise bad things, such as murder. It's regrettable, we say, but true.

But if we take the long view, starting with Gene Autry and ending with the latest version of a video such as Resident Evil 7 Biohazard, known affectionately to its fans as RE7, while throwing in the fact that there is now good evidence that violent video games of this nature are addictive, you can't help but see Queen Ego resurrected from the dead. The trend is growing. Violence, including mass shootings and terror attacks, is up. No movie worth its salt will win an Emmy if a car doesn't blow up somewhere along the line.

What's the cause of such activities? It starts with the word "I." "I" want be victorious. "I" want my way of life to be triumphant. "I" worship a God that is better than your God. "I" deserve more than I have. "I" was wronged.

"I" stands for Ego. So I hope you didn't cheer very loud when the evil queen got her comeuppance. I hope you could at least empathize a little with her plight. She was evil, yes. But she was also a victim of her own evil. Violence never redeemed anybody. The only way to kill her is to love her to death.

"But that's impossible and impractical in today's world," you say. "Where would we have been if we had allowed Hitler to rule the world? We had to meet his violence with an equal and even greater violence. Americans dropped the only two atomic bombs ever used in the history of warfare and destroyed millions of civilian non-combatants because it saved a lot of innocent lives. Americans were the good guys."

Yes, they were, then. There was probably no other way.

See how evil works? It places us in the center of a duality in which we are offered only two choices, both of which are tools that belong to ego.

And that's where the story suddenly ends. There is no wind-up, no explanation, and no morality lesson. The narrative just stops. "*She was forced to step into the red-hot shoes and dance until she fell down dead.*" Those are the final words in the saga of *Little Snow-White*.

How anticlimactic can you get? We were expecting a glorious finish, a "happily ever after" wedding or something. At the very least, we might have been left with a moral to the story. But we are met with deafening silence. We have run the race and there seems to be no finish line.

Is that bad story telling? Can we blame the author for leaving us high and dry?

Well, I suppose so. But the rest of the story was crafted so carefully we have to wonder if this, too, is intentional.

Perhaps the reason for this unsatisfying conclusion is that, for the most part, that's how life usually ends. Unless we die in a triumphant battle for truth over falsehood, waving a flag of righteousness while storming the ramparts of evil, our end usually comes not with a bang, but with a final, shallow sigh.

Most of us don't get a chance to completely fulfill our dreams. If we outlive our friends, there are few who come to mourn us. Tears are shed and fond words of memorial are offered, but then life goes on. People continue on with their lives.

Why should Snow-White be any different? She is, after all, just another character, playing a role in just another story. She is every-woman and every-man. She is us.

Like her, we are born of blood and water into a natural environment that forms a blank slate for our story. But like her, we are also immortal beings, here on the adventure of a lifetime. Like her, we shall someday be united with our prince, the "us on the other side," who will greet us when we depart this life. And our ego, the essential "I" who we must learn to control, lest it controls us, will go the way of all flesh.

And the story will begin again, as life goes on. The dance of death, it turns out, is not a pas de deux between Ego and Soul. It is Ego's final solo, dancing alone on the stage of life, to music she herself has composed.

Our royal wedding, so deserved and so anticipated, will take place in a land far, far better than we have ever seen in this life. It is not simply our reward. It is our destiny.

And the dance continues forever.

Conclusion

Befor we start forming any tentative conclusions about meanings to be drawn from this story, it's time to address some questions that have probably been in the back of your mind from the very beginning:

• "Did the original author of this story really understand all this stuff about Ego and Intuitive Innocence, the material world of nature and the Source?"

• "Did he or she carefully compose a parable that would encapsulate all of it?"

• "Was this the real purpose of the tale to begin with? If so, why disguise it?"

The answer to the sum of these questions is simple and direct: No, probably not.

But that doesn't mean that the conclusions we are about to draw are not there. The original authors didn't necessarily understand all the symbolism. They just wrote what sounded right. They tapped into the magic of the

Muse—which exists in a field of consciousness quite independent from human reality—and drew out meaning they probably didn't even understand themselves.

Let me try to explain it this way. Johann Sebastian Bach once famously said, "The aim and final end of all music should be none other than the glory of God and the refreshment of the soul." He didn't mean that all music should be church music. A lot of his music was never meant to be played in church. What he was saying was that he understood music is drawn from what can best be called a spiritual source, whether it's performed by a Gregorian Choir, Leonard Bernstein, John Lennon, or Willie Nelson. Music speaks to our feelings, not our intellect. And anything that makes us *feel*, rather than *think*, is obviously not simply a materialistic exercise.

That being said, however, Johann Sebastian Bach's music is some of the most basic, intellectual, one might almost say mechanical, glorious, music ever written. He summed up the entire Baroque Period and formed the rules that govern basic harmonic structures that are used in virtually every song you've ever heard.

When a classic blues group follows what is called a I, IV, V chord pattern, they are following rules laid down by J.S. Bach. When a jazz ensemble, composed of people who have never played together, or, for that matter, even met each other, sit down together to improvise, they can perform as a unified group because they all have Bach's harmonic structures in their heads. When groups such as the Beatles or the Rolling Stones composed and performed songs before huge audiences, they weren't thinking about Bach, but the old keyboardist could easily have sat in with them, because they were following rules he wrote down and systematized.

When I went to music school I, like every other classically trained musician who has lived during the last 500 years, spent years studying the chorales of Johann Sebastian Bach. So did everyone from Billy Joel to Chuck Mangione to John Batiste. Bach wrote the book. We needed to discover how he did it.

We learned, for instance, that notes comprising intervals of fourths, fifths, and octaves, should never move parallel to one another. A piece almost always needed to end on a tonic chord. Phrases should usually be eight measures long. The rules became second nature.

Sometimes people broke them on purpose, but it was always for a special effect. The classic song, *Yesterday*, for instance, by Paul McCartney of the Beatles, follows a typical song form called A/A/B/A. The "B" section is eight measures long. But the "A" sections are only seven measures long.

Why? Just to be different. But the difference stands out because we are so used to typically Bach-inspired patterns of eight-bar music. You don't have to understand what's going on in order to enjoy the song, but you usually hear when something out of the ordinary happens.

Was old Johann aware that he was such a pivotal musician? Of course not. He was just trying to make enough money to feed his family while satisfying his artistic nature. He didn't invent the rules. He discovered them. Once in a while he even broke them. But overall, he recognized that certain vibrational sequences caused a response in human sensibilities. He didn't compose only with his brain. He responded to his Muse. The result is something that has stood the test of time because his intellectual, systematic genius was a vehicle through which Akashic possibilities could manifest themselves. The rules were a means to an end.

All artists are like that, including the ones who wrote classic stories, such as *Little Snow-White*, that cause a response in the human psyche.

I'm no genius, by any means. But even I have had the experience of reading something I was inspired to write years ago, and suddenly felt as though I was reading it for the first time. Even though I wrote the original words, they sometimes seem to come alive with meaning I never intended, or at least didn't know I intended. It doesn't happen often. Not nearly as much as I wish it would. But it happens. And when it does, I know that, for a few minutes, when I was open and responsive, even I sometimes became a vehicle for inspiration.

That's what is going on as we read *Little Snow-White*. The author has touched the Muse, probably without even realizing it. In the preceding pages, I've brought out some meaning that perhaps the original author didn't overtly intend. But I'll bet you've found meaning that I missed—meaning that touches you in a way it hasn't yet touched me, because your life experience has been different from mine.

That's the mark of artistic genius. In the long run, the artist isn't really important. It's the art that counts. That's what lasts down through the generations that follow.

So let's draw some conclusions that might, or might not, have been in the mind of whoever first told this story, trusting that the mind of the story-teller isn't as important as the Source from which the story-teller drew.

Life is But a Dream

We begin with the story itself, independent from any interior meaning. Just the fact that it is still told is important, because it resonates with the human condition. It has joined a pantheon of small, independent pieces of art that shaped humanity in profound ways

A few years ago, while writing my book, *Supernatural Gods*, I had a brief insight into the meaning of a song that I hadn't sung for years. I'm sure you'll recognize it:

Row, row, row your boat, gently down the stream.

Merrily, merrily, merrily, merrily
Life is but a dream.

It's designed to be sung first by a single person. It starts out as a solo. But soon, a second person joins in, repeating the same melody. The two melodies are exactly the same, distinct only by the vocal timbre, or we might say, individual nuances, of the individual singers. But, sung in this fashion, they now form harmony. Then a third person joins in, and it continues. If you listen to each individual voice by itself, you'll hear the same song. But if you listen to them all together you hear a complex, harmonic composition. When the first singer finishes, he or she is symbolically reincarnated and begins again. After a while, the audience doesn't know who started to sing, who joined in second or third, or even how many times each musician has sung the whole song. It just continues on and on—a seemingly endless loop of individual expressions that, together, form a complex composition.

The message of the lyrics is especially important. The words remind us to propel our "boat," that is, the material body that houses our primal souls, down the stream of life. They remind us to be gentle with the craft that carries us through life. "Be merry," they say. "Take joy in your journey because, after all, life is but a dream.

Thus, we each sing the short little song of life. Each life is independent and stands alone. But together, as we each start at the beginning, singing what someone else has sung before, we build a great, harmonious chorus, with complex counterpoint and expression. When we finish our song, we return to the beginning, reincarnated, and sing it again.

In *Supernatural Gods* I summed up what this insight meant to me:

How many repetitions? I guess we just keep singing until we feel we are finished. Then we drop out and let others carry the score. It really doesn't matter. There's no hurry, because it's all happening inside us anyway. We create, and are creating, the whole universe. That's who we are — creators. And what of the individual lives we lead here, on this earth and maybe others as well? Don't worry. They're just a dream. Learn from them, but be gentle with yourselves while you do it. And be merry!

D.C. al Fine

Row, Row, Row Your Boat is a simple little ditty, but it carries profound meaning that the original composer might not have intended. And it's still around. People are still singing it, whether they discover meaning in it or not. Even children sing it. It becomes a part of their very fiber.

Little Snow-White is no different. Children may appreciate it as a bedtime story. Disney may find in its inspiration for a movie. When we engage a story such as this, we enter a dream world—a fantasy world. The very fact that it is so engaging and popular proves there is something lasting beneath the surface. All we have to do is think about it a little. There is reality found in that world, and it resonates with our human experience. As long as we are engaged, the wicked queen, the huntsman, the dwarfs, and Snow-White are real people who inhabit a real landscape. We identify with them. They have lessons to teach us.

That, in itself, is an important lesson. Because if a waking dream world can teach us about the meaning of our lives, what other dream worlds do the same thing? What about the dream world of our imaginations? What about the dream world we enter each night in sleep? What about the world of daydreams? Are they any more "real" than the world of waking consciousness?

Maybe the song is correct. Life *is* but a dream!

Ego and Our Narcissistic Age

Sometimes I think the central character of this story isn't Snow-White, but rather Queen Ego. In many ways, she's the one with whom I most identify. I say this because, like many people, I often find myself spending too much time in front of my own "mirror"—my computer screen, checking to see how many people emailed me or reading my latest social media post. From conversations I've had with others, it's apparently quite common these days. We stare at a screen, and see a reflection of ourselves. The computer thus becomes a mirror.

Social media! We love it and we hate it. It allows us to stay connected with old friends and catch up with the latest trends. But it also spotlights awful-sounding diatribes from angry people.

In some ways it reminds me of what the world was like back in 1491, the year before "Columbus sailed the ocean blue." His voyage kicked off what has been called the age of discovery. Up until then, oceans were barriers that separated people. Afterwards, within a very short time, those barriers turned into highways.

Make no mistake about it. There were tremendous benefits to sharing ideas and goods. There were immensely important intellectual breakthroughs when previously distinct cultures clashed together. Vastly expanding markets led to many, many improvements. In most ways, the world took a great leap forward.

But there were also devastating social, health, and cultural results that led to warfare, wholesale slaughter of entire populations, and devastating ecological destruction. Some individuals, even whole countries, benefited. Others suffered greatly and eventually disappeared.

That's social media in a nutshell. It offers great promise and great reward. It brings together people from many and varied locations.

But it is also a tool for those who, out of power-hungry ego, desire to hurt, manipulate, and even destroy.

No one is immune and the issue is not a black and white situation. Most of us are neither completely innocent nor completely guilty. That's how ego works. Remember, it utilizes disguise. We can be following its gleeful manipulations without even knowing it.

None of us are forced to habitually check our social media platforms. We do it because we want to. We would be appalled if Queen Ego suddenly jumped out of the bushes and ambushed us. But that's not how she works. She sneaks up on us, gradually and seductively. No one decided one day to start spending four or five hours a day in front of a computer screen. It happened gradually. That's Queen Ego's *modus operandi*. Little by little, day by day, she seduces us and sells us her wares. And we are only too anxious to buy her bill of goods.

It is only when we suddenly confront, to our horror, the hold she has on us, that we are sometimes able to break free. Alas, by that time we are often willing captives. It's not that we can't escape her clutches. It's that by the time we realize her hold on us, we don't want to.

The power of alcohol and drug addiction can only be broken when we are willing to stand up in public and admit to the world, "I am an alcoholic." In the same way, the power of ego gratification can only addressed when we are willing to admit its hold on us. Until then, ego holds all the cards.

Sad to say, there is ample evidence that these days she seems to be winning the game. But the second step in overcoming an addiction is to seek help from a High Power.

Help From Outside

In order to fully grasp the vast powers we are dealing with in the battle between Egotistic Individuality and Intuitive Innocence, we need to make a very important presumption. It is simply stated: *There is help available*!

Soul is eternal. Therefore, soul can rely on support from the country where it was born—the land of the Source.

I'm talking about spirituality. Soul is separate from body. It encapsulates a body during its sojourn on earth. It is not produced, owned, or otherwise captured by body. It has vast spiritual resources it can call on. An entire field of consciousness stands ready to help.

The prince lives in this field. It's his home country. But, if necessary, he will travel to the very portals of death in order to bring his beloved home.

Each and every one of us has such a princely spirit guide, a heavenly messenger, a guardian angel—call it what you will—watching over us. The spirit guide is the other part of ourselves that lives on the other side of materialistic reality. We may, for a time, live in ego's domain, but that world is temporary. Ego exists in the brief match snap of time between birth and death. Spirit is eternal.

The marriage between Snow-White and the Prince will take place. As we have seen, even on the way to a funeral, ancient Earth Energies that remember their Source stand ready to reach out, trip up the procession, and turn it into a celebration of life. We are never without hope.

Ego will someday dance its way to death and Intuitive Innocence will reap the reward which is its final destiny. When you are down in the dumps and wondering if you are totally alone and without resources in a cruel world, when all seems lost and you feel you are simply making your way to the doorstep of death, hold on to this hope with all your might. You may not feel it, but believe it anyway.

Alexander Pope said it well:

Hope springs eternal in the human breast;
Man never Is, but always To be blest.
The soul, uneasy, and confin'd from home,
Rests and expatiates in a life to come.

The story of *Little Snow-White* thus reminds us that even when confronting what appears to be an end—death itself—we are not without resources. The huntsman played his part. The dwarfs, Keepers of the Sacred Flame, played their part. The prince arrived at the right time. The whole time, Queen Ego was outnumbered and surrounded. She just didn't know it. She never had a chance. In the end, she was defeated.

And through it all, Snow-White maintained her innocence.

So shall it always be.

Acknowledgements

I was two-thirds finished writing this book when, in the course of my research, I came across a book by Ryan Holiday called *Ego is the Enemy*. I'm glad I was so close to the end of this project when I read it. Holiday's book is so powerful it might have intimidated me enough so as to keep me from ever starting. I've never met him, although it is my fondest wish that someday the two of us will be able to sit down for a good, long talk. Ryan, if these words ever find their way to you, thank you!

The late Joseph Campbell, after his teaching career had ended, and he thought he was done sharing his wisdom with his students, was rediscovered when gatekeepers such as George Lucas and Bill Moyers breathed fresh life into his work and presented him afresh to a new audience, who otherwise would never have heard of him. He must have felt as though he was cast out into the wilderness when a very few influential Huntsmen caused his light to shine as it never had before. That's when I met him on television and was changed forever. We all were. Myth was reborn in popular consciousness. We should all be forever grateful.

To those who have contributed in ways large and small to my personal search for meaning beneath the surface of things, I am forever grateful. You are all Keepers of the Sacred Flame!

Further Reading

Ashton, John and Tom Whyte. *The Quest for Paradise: Visions of Heaven and Eternity in the World's Myths and Religions*. New York, NY: Harper Collins, 2001.

Bullfinch's Mythology. New York, NY: Gramercy Books, 1979

Campbell, Joseph with Bill Moyers. *The Power of Myth*. New York, NY: Bantam, Doubleday Dell Publishing Group, 1988.

Campbell, Joseph. *Transformations of Myth through Time*. New York, NY: Harper and Row, 1990.

Dennett, Daniel. *Darwin's Dangerous Idea: Evolution and the Meanings of Life*. New York, NY: Touchstone, 1996.

Felser, Joseph M. *The Way Back to Paradise: Restoring the Balance Between Magic and Reason*. Charlottesville, VA: Hampton Roads Publishing Co., 2005.

Fisher, Mary Pat and Lee W. Bailey. *An Anthology of Living Religions*. Upper Saddle River, NJ: Prentiss Hall, 2000.

Harner, Michael. *Cave and Cosmos*. Berkeley, CA: North Atlantic Books, 2013.

Harner, Michael. *The Way of the Shaman*. San Francisco, CA: Harper & Row, 1980.

Nick Herbert. *Quantum Reality*. New York, NY: Random House, 1985.

Highwater, Jamake. *The Primal Mind: Vision and Reality in Indian America*. New York, NY: Harper & Row Publishers, Inc., 1981.

Hitching, Francis. *Earth Magic*. New York, NY: William Morrow and Company, Inc., 1977.

Holiday, Ryan. *Ego is the Enemy*. New York, NY: Portfolio/Penguin, an imprint of Random House LLC, 2016.

James, Simon. *The World of the Celts*. London, England: Thames and Hudson LTD, 1993.

Kauffman, Stuart A. *Reinventing the Sacred: A New View of Science, Reason, and Religion*. Philadelphia, PA: Basic Books, 2008.

Laszlo, Ervin. *Science and the Akashic Field: An Integral Theory of Everything, Updated Second Edition*. Rochester, VT.: Inner Traditions, 2007.

Laszlo, Ervin. *The Akashic Experience: Science and the Cosmic Memory Field*. Rochester, VT: Inner Traditions, 2009.

Laszlo, Ervin. *The Whispering Pond: A Personal Guide to the Emerging Vision of Science*. Rockport, MA: Element Books, Inc., 1996.

Mails, Thomas E. *Dancing in the Paths of the Ancestors*. New York, NY: Marlowe & Co.

Rolleston, T. W. *Myths & Legends of the Celtic Race*. London, England, The Ballantine Press.

Sagan, Carl. *The Dragons of Eden*. New York, NY: Ballantine Books, 1977.

Willis, Jim. *The Religion Book: Places, Prophets, Saints and Seers*. Detroit, MI: Visible Ink Press, 2004.

Willis, Jim. *Supernatural Gods: Spiritual Mysteries, Psychic Experiences and Scientific Truths*. Detroit, MI: Visible Ink Press, 2017.

About the Author

The author of thirteen books, ranging from ancient religion and 21st century spirituality to long-distance bicycle riding, he has been an ordained minister for over forty years, while working part-time as a carpenter, the host of his own drive-time radio show, an arts council director, and adjunct college professor in the fields of World Religions and Instrumental Music.

Other Books By Jim Willis

- Journey Home: The Inner Life of a Long-Distance Bicycle Rider
- The Religion Book: Places, Prophets, Saints, and Seers
- Armageddon Now: The End of the World A to Z
- Faith, Trust, & Belief: A Trilogy of the Spirit
- Snapshots and Visions: A View from the Now
- The Dragon Awakes: Rediscovering Earth Energy in the Age of Science
- Savannah: A Bicycle Journey Through Space and Time
- Lost Civilizations: The Secret Histories and Suppressed Technologies of the Ancients
- Ancient Gods: Lost Histories, Hidden truths, and the Conspiracy of Silence
- Supernatural Gods: Spiritual Mysteries, Psychic Experiences and Scientific Truths
- Hidden History: Ancient Aliens and the Suppressed Origins of Civilization
- The Quantum Akashic Field: A Guide to Out-of-Body Experiences for the Astral Traveler
- Censoring God: The History of the Lost Books

See www.jimwillis.net for reviews and ordering details.